Effective Everyday Evangelism: The Adventures Of Joe Clevelander & Chuck Churchman

Douglas E. Dingley

James Kay Publishing

Tulsa, Oklahoma

Effective Everyday Evangelism:
The Adventures of
Joe Clevelander & Chuck Churchman
ISBN 978-1-943245-14-7

www.jameskaypublishing.com
e-mail: sales@jameskaypublishing.com

© 2017 Douglas E. Dingley
Cover design by JKP
Cover Art courtesy of
Al Shannon: biblicalproof.wordpress.com

also by
Douglas E. Dingley

More Than Conquerors

Clearing Up The Confusion
The Cup; The Cross; and The Chaos!

**All Scripture references taken from
the New King James Version
unless otherwise noted.**

**Free 8 ½ x 11 downloads
of the bible studies
found in the back of this book,
as well as hundreds
of other biblically sound resources,
can be accessed on Doug's website at:
<u>www.Godswordistruth.org</u>**

A Brief Personal Note from the Author:

In Ephesians 4:11-16, God's Word says: *"And He Himself gave some to be apostles, some prophets, some evangelists, and some pastors and teachers, for the equipping of the saints for the work of ministry, for the edifying of the body of Christ, till we all come to the unity of the faith and of the knowledge of the Son of God, to a perfect man, to the measure of the stature of the fullness of Christ; that we should no longer be children, tossed to and fro and carried about with every wind of doctrine, by the trickery of men, in the cunning craftiness of deceitful plotting, but, speaking the truth in love, may grow up in all things into Him who is the head--Christ-- from whom the whole body, joined and knit together by what every joint supplies, according to the effective working by which every part does its share, causes growth of the body for the edifying of itself in love."*

While the church today no longer has anyone who is qualified or defined by God as being an "apostle" (Acts 1:21-2:3; 2nd Cor. 12:11-12); and while the church today is also a truly "non-prophet" organization; it is the "soul-responsibility" of today's evangelists, pastors, and teachers, to equip, prepare, edify, unify, educate, and encourage everyone in the congregation of God's saints whom they are blessed to serve and have been entrusted with by Him (Hebrews 13:17) to get out there and save precious souls, daily expanding the kingdom of Christ with His priceless gospel. It is my hope and prayer that what you are about to read will accomplish that and help further all your efforts in that area. To God be the glory; always and in all ways!

Table of Contents

cont.

Chapter One:

The Birth of 'Joe Clevelander' and 'Chuck Churchman'

One of the chief reasons for the very establishment and existence of the Lord's church is evangelism; the saving of lost souls; for, God "desires all men to be saved and to come to the knowledge of the truth" (1st Timothy 2:4). He is "not willing that any should perish but that all should come to repentance" (2nd Peter 3:9). The Lord Jesus Christ Himself, the Word made flesh who came and dwelt among us said during His earthly ministry that He came "to seek and to save the lost" (Luke 19:10). And one of the last things He did before He ascended back to glory was to give His hand-picked and chosen Apostles (and us by extension of course) the precious and glorious privilege of being His divinely-designated co-workers and sharers of that great 'co-mission' with Him when He said, "Go therefore and make disciples of all the nations, baptizing them in the name of the Father and of the Son and of the Holy Spirit, teaching them to observe all things that I have commanded you; and lo, I am with you always, even to the end of the age" (Matthew 28:19-20).

Indeed, as the divinely-inspired and Spirit-driven apostle Paul wrote to the first century congregation of the Lord's church that worked and worshipped in Thessalonica: "But as we have been approved by God to be entrusted with the gospel, even so we speak, not as pleasing men, but God who tests our hearts" (1st Thessalonians 2:4). The apostle Paul again echoed those same sentiments (that the ultimate reason for the church's very existence is for evangelistic purposes) when he wrote to the first century congregation of the Lord's church that worked and worshiped in Ephesus. There, in Ephesians 3, verses 8-12, he let both them and the entire world know in no uncertain terms, that the "eternal purpose" and crowning touch of God's plan from before the very beginning of time, was to establish His Son's one, New Testament church, and that it could make known the good news of Christ to a lost and dying world. This, so that the lost in sin world might receive it, believe it, obey it, live it, and be saved by it as well, thus being added by God to that grace-cleansed, blood-bought, and heaven-bound group; for God is "not willing that any should perish but that all should come to repentance" (2nd Peter 3:9)!

But how exactly do we most efficiently and effectively spread that grace-laden, soul-saving message of gospel truth – especially in today's fast-paced, immediate-gratification, instant electronic communication, "that's just your interpretation," media-saturated, satanically-infiltrated, religious diversity-celebrated, "no such thing as God or sin" world?

It was March of 2009 when my wife and I were blessed by God to come to the little town of Cleveland, Oklahoma, to work and worship within the small group of saints who labored there to extend and expand the one New Testament church of Christ (or Kingdom of God on earth - Matthew 16:18-19; Romans 16:16; and Colossians 1:13). Within a few months of our arrival I was encouraged to begin writing a short article which was to be published each week in our local newspaper. All in all, we published approximately one-hundred very thoroughly researched, very biblically footnoted, and very scripturally-concentrated articles… ***all to no avail*** - or so it seemed at the time of their cancellation due to a lack of public response (although one man from the community did come to us and to Christ some months after their cancellation as a result of their publication). Over the precise two-year period of their publication, the public's response aside from that one man's, didn't seem too dissimilar to that of the non-existent and false god 'Baal' from 1st Kings 18:29: "But there was no voice; no one answered, [and] no one paid attention."

So, what happened? What went wrong? Weren't the articles true? Yes! Weren't they biblical? Absolutely! Then why didn't more lost souls respond? Was it really true, as some of my contemporaries might concede, that there is just no interest in knowing God anymore amongst the lost and misled masses? I don't buy it. I've seen way too many people in way too many situations – both good and bad – who exhibit an extended desire to know God, His Son, and His Word, to even begin to believe that. So once again, what happened?

I believe the key to our understanding what might or might not work, 'for better or for worse' when it comes to efficient and effective evangelism today, begins with understanding, accepting, and internalizing Acts 8:35. In that particular passage, Phillip had been called down towards Gaza to evangelize an Ethiopian eunuch who was just returning home from a long trip up to worship in Jerusalem. A few elements of this encounter that should not escape our notice would include the fact that this eunuch was a deeply devoted and devoutly religious man – even though his devotion was to a religious system that God no longer honored after His Son's crucifixion on Calvary and the establishment of His one, New Testament church some fifty days after His resurrection (2nd Corinthians 3:4-16; Colossians 2:14; Hebrews, chapters 7-9; Acts, chapters 1 and 2). This should be of extreme importance to us because so often times we seem to think that those around us who are devoutly devoted to "their church," or "their home denomination," are not ever going to listen to, or ever be interested in, or ever be converted by, the gospel truth, exactly as it appears in God's Word.

We tend to forget that many of the most familiar examples of conversion to Christ in the book of Acts were all of people who had already shown a deep interest in God as evidenced by their already being very religious – although not of the "one faith" (Ephesians 4:4-6) - people! From the 3,000 devout Jews converted on the Day of Pentecost, to Saul of Tarsus, to Cornelius and his household, to Lydia and others, all of those converts obviously came from religions other than Christianity. And all of them can be shown to have been very pious and devoted thereto, prior to their having been presented with the whole counsel of God. And this Ethiopian eunuch was certainly no exception. Deeply devoted to his faith, he had traveled all the way from Ethiopia in Africa, up to Jerusalem in Israel to worship – even though as a eunuch he was not allowed past the court of the Gentiles (Deuteronomy 23:1). That's devotion, folks! Especially when we consider that some today can't seem to ride ten minutes in the air-conditioned, tinted windowed, G.P.S. guided, modern day automobile of their choice to the church building to worship with any sort of consistent Sunday regularity. On his way back home, even as he was riding and/or resting in his chariot throughout this dust-choked and deserted region, he was reading and studying the divinely-inspired words of the prophet Isaiah.

But as devoted as he is to his current religion when Phillip arrives and comes up alongside to 'discuss bible' with him, he is, very shortly thereafter, baptized into, and converted to Christ. How did this happen? What was Phillip's recipe for success? (Because let's face it folks, not many such discussions end as well or productively today - with the conversion of the conversant.) It ended the way it did, with the eunuch's conversion to Christ, due largely in part, to the way the discussion began…

As the eunuch sat reading from his quite-possibly-recently-purchased-in-Jerusalem copy of the scroll of Isaiah the prophet, the bible says in verse 35, that "Then Phillip opened his mouth, and beginning at this Scripture, preached Jesus to him." Did you catch that? I am completely convinced that that's the key to successful evangelism! We must follow Phillip's phenomenally successful example of personal evangelism by taking people from WHERE THEY ARE CURRENTLY AT, to where they eternally need to be, via the vehicle of the soul-saving Word of God and nothing less!

This is how the Lord Jesus, the Master Teacher modeled effective teaching throughout the gospels. This is what the apostle Paul did as he sought to "reason" with people as evidenced throughout much of the Book of Acts, wherein he constantly "reasoned" with – and saw converted – many of those people who held strong religious convictions but in a completely contrarian direction prior to his arrival to "talk religion" and "reason" with them as he presented the biblical doctrine of the grace-laden gospel of Christ to them (See: Acts 17:1-4, 10-12, 17; 18:4, 19; and 24:10-25.)

The fact is, that if we would be as truly and efficiently effective and successful as the Lord wants us to be when it comes to our evangelistic efforts, we must learn to integrate and emulate this example, so much so that it becomes second nature to us! We must learn to take people from WHERE

THEY ARE CURRENTLY AT, to where they eternally need to be, via the soul-saving Word of God and nothing less!

Looking back, a portion of the lack of fruit production from the newspaper paper articles might well have been due to their lack of such PERSONAL, biblically-patterned evangelism. I believe that that's the problem with far too many of our unsuccessful attempts and programs of evangelism today! They may 'well' be, some of the most well-intentioned, well-supported, well-attended, and/or well-funded attempts at personal and congregational outreach and evangelism that we can possibly put together, but if they don't reach the lost, where they are, on their level, FIRST, then they're probably not going to be, 'well,' very successful now are they? In fact, they will be more like a very unsuccessful 'well' – a deep, dark, empty, and unproductive hole, into which one pours resources without much to show for their efforts. Hence: the "birth" of "Joe Clevelander" and "Chuck Churchman."

"Joe Clevelander" is the name given to a fictitious character that was designed to give the average, local, "Joe Q. Public," or "Joe on the street" in our little town of Cleveland, someone to truly and fully identify with. As such, he is the cumulative mouthpiece for all of those crass, critical, skeptical, and/or sometimes quite unkind comments that are so often heard from the biblically ignorant and scripturally uninformed of our communities regarding the faithful members, biblical doctrines, God-fearing practices, and God-honoring obedience of the churches of Christ (Romans 16:16). In Joe, it is all laid right out there – tangibly, truthfully, and transparently. He sincerely voices some of the most common and recurring criticisms regularly leveled at the Lord's church today by the biblically uninformed religious zealots and denominational regulars permeating almost any community in modern-day America. Paul dealt with the same in the ancient world as well (Romans 10:2-3).

The fictitious "Chuck Churchman" however, is intended to be the epitome and example of what so many of us in the Lord's church, at least **_used to be_**. Well-studied, unflappable, and full of just good old common sense to boot, he knows his bible and how to rightly divide it (2ⁿᵈ Timothy 2:15), as well as how to appropriately apportion, argue, reason and apply it.

Automatically understanding and adjusting to the fact that he is not dealing with a decades-long, well-studied and well-informed member of the Lord's church in his friend Joe, and subsequently integrating the absolutely essential example of Acts 8:35 into his evangelistic efforts in order to make them as successful as they can possibly be, he consciously and consistently strives not to choke with the meat of the Word, one who is not yet even ready for the milk of the Word, not having even entered into infancy in the family of God yet by being "born again" of the water and the Spirit (John 3:3-5). Instead, Chuck seeks to **illustrate through common, everyday examples**, the uncommon, incredible, and eternal truths of God's instruction in a way that Joe can understand and easily accept and process. This is the same exact thing that Jesus did, as He effectively taught the people about heavenly and eternal truths, with simple, everyday, earthly terms like "fish," "fishermen," "baskets," "rocks," "salt," and "light" – items which every lost soul in earshot could quite easily understand, being ultimately and intimately familiar with them from their everyday lives.

"Chuck" also understands that, as his preacher has repeatedly proclaimed countless times, it is not his job to convert anyone. That is God's job (1st Corinthians 3:5-9). Chuck's only job is to plant the seed of the Word in the soil of Joe's heart so that God can do what He does best, and that, through the implanted Word (cf. Luke 8:4-11; James 1:22-23). That is why, as you will hopefully note, that "Chuck" constantly, relentlessly, and aggressively keeps trying to get Joe into the bible with a regularly-scheduled bible study and attendance at worship services. He gives him just enough scripture to answer his questions, but continually invites Joe to study further - because the more Joe is in the Word, the more of the Word will get into Joe (2nd Peter 1:2-12)!

And a third thing you will hopefully note about "Chuck's" approach, is that he constantly asks questions. He makes Joe really, seriously, and thoroughly consider his long-held but biblically erroneous convictions. One of Chuck's favorite phrases, mottos, and mindsets – whether ever verbalized or not - is that "Good teachers ask questions." That's how the Master Teacher Jesus so often and effectively taught, and if it was good enough for His Master, then it's good enough for Chuck Churchman – who hopefully represents and epitomizes all of us who are faithful and obedient members of Christ's one New Testament church as seen in Scripture.

These are just some of the timeless secrets to successful evangelism that so many of us have maybe either forgotten somewhere along the way, or perhaps were possibly never taught in the first place... and so, the Lord's church and cause has continually suffered, being somewhat less successful at soul-saving than maybe we all could have been on occasion.

This is the reason for this writing; to take us back to the basics of both biblical AND automatic common sense answers and applications when confronted by those who only think they know what the bible actually says, so that we can perhaps convert them to Christ and help them to come to a better and fuller knowledge of the truth. As Christians, this is our God-given mission. This must be our primary passion. And we must bring it as close as we can to complete perfection!

> "And a servant of the Lord must not quarrel but be gentle to all, able to teach, patient, in humility correcting those who are in opposition, if God perhaps will grant them repentance, so that they may know truth, and that they may come to their senses and escape the snare of the devil, having been taken captive by him to do his will" (2nd Timothy 2:24-26).

> "And on some have compassion, making a distinction; but others save with fear, pulling them out of the fire, hating even the garment defiled by the flesh" (Jude 1:22-23).

But how do we patiently, lovingly, and compassionately get the often critical, confused, and confrontational lost of our world to where they need to be scripturally, and eventually then, on into Christ? How do we "confront without being confrontational?" For example, in a world where people at least generally claim to believe that they shouldn't rush to judgment about anything or anyone – and especially not until they have all of the obtainable facts in hand – what a complete contradiction they have been known to sometimes practice when it comes to members of the churches of Christ! You've probably either heard it said, or perhaps even had it spat in your face when discussing with someone the fact that you are a member of the church of Christ, that, "Oh yeah, you're the bunch that thinks you're the only ones going to heaven!" This charge is sometimes made by somewhat well-intentioned denominational religious people, who then summarily dismiss any further positive discussion of the church of Christ folks and their biblical beliefs and convictions, based on what they themselves have instantly and inadvertently '**judged**,' to be the inappropriate 'judgmentalism' on the part of those church of Christ folks!

But in reality, when discussed more deeply, most denominational folks – and even the general (non-atheist) populace at large – will eventually come to understand and be forced to admit that their own thinking isn't all that far off from what the church of Christ folks actually believe – **if we handle it right**. But how do we do that? How do we handle the charge that we "think we're the only ones going to heaven," when hurled venomously at us by those who have judged **us** to be too judgmental? By those who have themselves, excluded us from any serious spiritual consideration because they have judged **us** to be too exclusive and or "narrow-minded?"

We certainly can't point out the blatant hypocrisy and double standard of their judgmental position to them, as that would surely shut down any further opportunity for productive conversation. That would also be unkind and un-Christ-like (Matthew 5:38-48; Luke 23:34). And we also certainly can't deny the Lord and His Word (Mark 8:38) which teaches us unequivocally that His church is simply all the sinners He has saved by His blood (Acts 20:28; 2:38-47), and that subsequently, the 'saved of Christ's' are 'the church of Christ.' The bible clearly teaches that these two terms are perfectly synonymous and that any soul outside of either is soon to be entering into the eternal inferno.

But at the same time, how do we feed that spiritual "meat" to those who haven't even been born again into the family (John 3:3-5; Galatians 3:26-27) so as not to even be able to handle such spiritual "milk" yet (1st Peter 2:1-3)? How do we handle with care and lovingkindness, those who attack us with pure relentlessness, while neither attacking back or giving them legitimate grounds to further judge us as too judgmental?

Answer: We must be, as Jesus put it, as "wise as serpents and harmless as doves" (Matthew 10:16).

For the sake of illustration, please carefully consider the following fictitious – although hopefully, very accurate to reality – conversations, as they could (and should) occur in "Anytown, U.S.A.," on any given day, between your average "Joe" on the street, and "Chuck," who is a faithful member of the local congregation of the church of Christ (Romans 16:16) nearest you…

Chapter One Questions for Classroom Discussion

1) How important is it to God that we seek to evangelize every, single, sinner we know, according to and in light of such passages as Luke 19:10, 1st Timothy 2:4, and 2nd Peter 3:9?

2) Please explain the infinite significance of Acts 8:35 when it comes to initiating effective evangelism today.

3) Do the examples of conversion to Christ we have in the book of Acts involve those who were already "religious" (i.e., already involved in and devoted to a religion other than Christianity before the full and true gospel was preached to them), or, people who had no previous interest in religion whatsoever? What should that help us to understand when it comes to evangelism?

4) Please explain how "Chuck Churchman's" evangelistic methods mimic and parallel the teaching techniques modeled by our Lord and Savior, the Master Teacher, Jesus Christ.

5) Please complete, and then discuss the implications of, the following two sentences:

   • 'Chuck' understands that it is not his job to _____ anyone. (What is his/our job?)

   • One of Chuck's favorite phrases, mottos, and mindsets – whether ever verbalized or not - is that 'Good teachers _____ _____.'

6) How did you respond the last time someone you loved enough to speak the biblical truth to, judged you as being too "judgmental," simply because you sought to share the soul-saving and grace-laden gospel message of repentance and baptism with them?

7) If one were to ever seek to somehow feed a big, tough, piece of steak to either a newborn - or more incredible yet, an unborn - baby, what would inevitably happen? Please explain how this preposterous but deadly scenario would apply when talking about perhaps seeking to evangelize by feeding big, tough, spiritual truth to a person who hasn't even been spiritually born (born again) yet, into the family of God.

NOTES

NOTES

Chapter Two:

The Only Ones Going to Heaven?

"Hey Joe, how's it going?" Chuck asked, as he saw one of the guys he recognized from work walking out of the corner convenience store. They had visited briefly before while standing in line at the office cafeteria but that was about it.

"It's going okay I guess," Joe responded in a friendly manner, not knowing too much about Chuck at all, except that he seemed to be a genuinely friendly 'nice guy.' "Hey," Joe added, "I really wanted to let you know how nice it was to see someone praying over their meal like I noticed you doing yesterday in the cafeteria. [1] You don't see that much anymore."

"No, I guess you don't. But God is the center of my life and I believe all good things come from Him and so I always strive to say, 'Thank You,' [2] like our preacher said we should in Sunday school class last week," Chuck said.

"Oh yeah? You go to church?" Joe questioned. That didn't seem all that surprising. In fact, it seemed to make sense from everything he'd seen of Chuck. Chuck nodded. "What church do you go to?" Joe followed up quickly but a bit tentatively. He and his family had been hoping to find some sincerely bible-believing and practicing place to worship, and one that took God's Word very seriously since their moving into town some months ago. But they had been exercising caution and not hurrying it because they were sick and tired of the "spiritual entertainment spiral" and were more interested in really learning and exploring what the bible actually said and meant rather than just simply being spiritually entertained anymore.[3]

"We attend worship with the rest of the Cleveland church of Christ over on Delaware Street," Chuck responded without hesitation.[4]

Oh no, not them, Joe thought. And before he could bite his tongue and catch himself, he had blurted out a thought implanted in his head since childhood by his extremely religious older brother: "That's the bunch that believes they're the only ones going to heaven, right?"

Chuck, completely unruffled and unsurprised by this not unanticipated response, simply said, "Actually, we probably don't believe too awfully differently on that than you yourself really do Joe."

Somewhat surprised, suddenly challenged, and more than just a little bit taken aback himself by Chuck's totally unexpected and unruffled response, Joe simply but somewhat nervously stuttered, "How so?" And as Chuck calmly and quietly responded, it would probably have been an understatement to say that he had Joe's complete and undivided attention!

"Well, do you believe that Jesus is the Son of God and that only He can save you just like He said in John 14:6?" Chuck asked.

Joe nodded.

"Well, so do we," Chuck calmly said. "Do you believe that only those saved by, of, and through the sacrificial blood of Jesus Christ Himself will be in heaven?" [5]

Joe thought for a moment about where this might be going and then nodded in agreement once again.

"So, do we," Chuck said. "And do you believe that in order to go to heaven, one must receive the gift of eternal life by accepting God's and Christ's sacrificial gift of grace on Their terms?" [6] Chuck asked, now intently looking Joe straight in the eye.

Once again, Joe nodded in complete agreement. After all, how could he not? He had spent enough time reading His bible to know that one must have faith enough in what God said, to submit themselves to God's will and accept His gift of grace in order to be saved. It made no sense to him whatsoever that it all just happened arbitrarily, or pre-birth, and that there was nothing anyone could do about it either way the way some churches taught. If that were the case, then why did God bother to divinely inspire so many of His handpicked writers to put so much in the scriptures regarding repentance, living the new life, and bettering one's previously unholy behavior?

"Hmmm," Chuck sighed after a momentary silence, "Imagine that; that's exactly what we believe too! So, let me see if I've got this straight... You believe that the only way a person can be truly saved, is by God's plan, Christ's blood, and God's grace, through that person's own faith... which would of course involve, believing what God said in His Word enough to submit to His terms and conditions for accepting His grace? Does that about sum it up?" Chuck asked. "Because if so, then you seem to believe about the same way as we do from what I can see," Chuck said, smiling slightly.

"...Yes," Joe replied somewhat hesitantly, now quite intrigued by what he had just learned in this little 'chance' (?) encounter.

"Do you know what God's Word actually states those terms and conditions for receiving His grace and forgiveness actually are?" Chuck added. "Because those are obviously vital to know – believing what you just said you do and all."

"All I have to do is believe," Joe stated quickly and not a little bit uncomfortably. After all, even though he had never been completely convinced of the "faith only saves" position, he had heard it preached many times from many denominational pulpits.

"Tell you what," Chuck continued; "James, chapter two would probably add a little bit of insight into that answer. Do you know what God says there?"

Joe shook his head. "

It says in verse 19," Chuck continued, "that 'even the demons believe – and shudder.' It goes on to say, in the only passage in the entire New Testament where the phrase 'faith only' is found, that justification is '*not* by faith only,' in verse 24. But please don't take my word for it – go home and check it out for yourself in your own copy of God's Word and see what you find. You do believe what Jesus said in John 17:17 about God's Word being the truth I assume?"

Joe muttered a quick "Yes, of course I do," while his mind whirled about and sought to process this new information which no denominational preacher, friend, his older brother, or anyone else had ever pointed out to him before. He actually wondered for a moment if Chuck had any idea what he was talking about, or was he just pulling his leg...? That statement about salvation ***not*** being by 'faith only' couldn't possibly, actually be in the bible there in James two…could it? At least, he had never seen it. He would have to check it out. And all of the sudden it hit Joe as to just how little of the Bible (for a semi-regular… well, maybe 'occasional' would be a better word …church-goer) that he actually knew himself, and just how vital it was to his spiritual well-being to know maybe a little more…

As if able to read his newly-confused thoughts, Chuck invited Joe to come over to his house and join them for Bible study that very evening, or even this coming Sunday with the rest of the local church of Christ. "But be forewarned, we don't do entertainment," Chuck quickly added. "There's enough of that all around us already on a daily basis… and besides, time is all too fleeting and all too precious to waste it being entertained when there's so much in God's Word we all need to learn. [7] And so, it's all about 'book, chapter, and verse' when we get together for worship and study. You're always welcome to join us, and we always learn something new from the Word of God. Love to have you Joe; you can sit with my family. Might we see you tonight, or even perhaps there on Sunday?"

ENDNOTES:

1. **1ˢᵗ Timothy 4:1-5:** Now the Spirit expressly says that in latter times some will depart from the faith, giving heed to deceiving spirits and doctrines of demons, speaking lies in hypocrisy, having their own conscience seared with a hot iron, forbidding to marry, *and commanding* to abstain from foods which God created to be received with thanksgiving by those who believe and know the truth. For every creature of God *is* good, and nothing is to be refused if it is received with thanksgiving; for it is sanctified by the word of God and prayer.

2. **1ˢᵗ Thessalonians 5:16-18:** Rejoice always, pray without ceasing, in everything give thanks; for this is the will of God in Christ Jesus for you.

3. **Ephesians 5:15-17:** See then that you walk circumspectly, not as fools but as wise, redeeming the time, because the days are evil. Therefore do not be unwise, but understand what the will of the Lord *is*.

4. **Matthew 10:32-33:** "Therefore whoever confesses Me before men, him I will also confess before My Father who is in heaven. But whoever denies Me before men, him I will also deny before My Father who is in heaven."

   Mark 8:38: "For whoever is ashamed of Me and My words in this adulterous and sinful generation, of him the Son of Man also will be ashamed when He comes in the glory of His Father with the holy angels."

   Acts 4:12: Nor is there salvation in any other, for there is no other name under heaven given among men by which we must be saved."

5. **Romans 5:9:** Much more then, having now been justified by His blood, we shall be saved from wrath through Him."

6. **<u>Mark 16:15-16:</u>** And He said to them, "Go into all the world and preach the gospel to every creature. He who believes and is baptized will be saved; but he who does not believe will be condemned.

7. **<u>Ephesians 5:15-17:</u>** See then that you walk circumspectly, not as fools but as wise, redeeming the time, because the days are evil. Therefore do not be unwise, but understand what the will of the Lord *is*.

Chapter Two Questions for Classroom Discussion

1) How important is the proper, daily, biblical example, if we are to evangelize the world around us?

2) Read Titus 2:1-10 and explain what it means to properly "adorn the doctrine of God our Savior in all things." Give personal examples.

3) How long did it take Chuck to integrate "God," "Sunday school," and "church" into his conversation with his co-worker? How long should it take us?

4) Please read 1st Peter 3:13-17 and apply its teaching to Chuck's mindset and priorities.

5) Describe what is meant by the 'spiritual entertainment spiral' and why it is 'never enough.'

6) Please read/study Mark 8:38, Romans 1:16, and 1st Peter 4:14-17. What is the common thread/word found within all of those verses and what does it mean? Describe how it did or didn't apply to Chuck, and then discuss how you think Jesus regards about those today who want to change the designation of their congregation from "------ church of Christ" to some other term of reference such as "-----Community Church," etc.

7) What was Solomon's counsel when it came to how we are to handle criticism (Proverbs 15:1-2)?

8) What was Jesus' response when reviled for righteousness (1st Peter 2:19-24)? How was Chuck's response similar?

9) Chuck's favorite phrase when it came to effective teaching was, "Good teachers _____ _____."

10) How did Chuck handle confrontation and questions without being confrontational and arrogant? With what qualities does God's Word say His teachers must handle their obligations in conveying the Word He gave them, in 2nd Timothy 2:22-26?

11) What have you personally learned from Chuck's methods, and how do you plan to put these lessons into practice?

Chapter Three:

Of Pearls, Puzzles, and Pianos

What a beautiful Saturday morning, Joe thought as he pulled into Fedoya Park for his oldest daughter's soccer game. (The coaches had requested the girls all be there a bit earlier than usual for warm-ups.) As he parked the car and his wife and two daughters piled out with soccer equipment in tow, he noticed that his co-worker, Chuck, and his family were already there. Chuck was the "church of Christ guy" from work whom Joe always enjoyed talking to about the Bible because Chuck seemed to know it so well, and yet at the same time, didn't come across like an arrogant "know it all."

After Joe collected the two lawn chairs from the rear of his truck, he waved his wife over and then approached where Chuck was sitting. He had been particularly perturbed lately and at a loss to understand something he had heard about the churches of Christ. Hoping for an answer, he went over and set up his and his wife's chairs beside where Chuck and his family were sitting.

Eventually, after the introductions and obligatory weather and game comments had concluded, Joe quietly and, due to his own unfamiliarity, a bit sheepishly said, "Hey, Chuck; I've got a question for you... I've heard it said recently that churches of Christ don't have... music... is that true?"

Chuck smiled and responded jovially, "No, that's not true at all – not even remotely. We enjoy some of the sweetest and finest worship music ever sung. Every Christian there – young and old alike – seeks to pour out their praises in song to God with all their heart, mind, and soul just the way God commanded His faithful New Testament church to do so long ago."

"That's not quite what I meant," Joe responded wryly. "I meant, is it true that you guys don't use instruments? All the other churches do. Are you saying they're wrong?"

Without missing a beat, Chuck said, "What I'm saying is this… Let's suppose your wife, whom you love deeply, has made it abundantly clear that she wants one particular pearl necklace from you for her special day. She has carefully placed a color picture of it beside your alarm clock so that it's the first thing you see when you wake up in the morning. She has meticulously pasted a picture of it on your medicine cabinet mirror so that when you go in to shave you can't miss it. Coming down the stairs for breakfast, you see that she has slid a picture of it halfway under your breakfast plate – as well as another under your coffee cup. Leaving for work and getting into your car, you see that she has additionally placed a picture of it in front of your speedometer – this one, complete with the cost, catalogue number, and store location details for your convenience. And finally, picking up your cell phone to text her that "OK, OK, you got the message already," you see that she has posted a picture of it on there as your wallpaper! That's six, different, unmistakable messages, indicating exactly what she wants on her special day. And so, the question then becomes: Do you love her enough to give her what she asked for? Or, do you suppose it would be "just fine" with her if you got her a purple, plaid, silk, man's necktie instead? After all, they both go around the neck."

"Not if he knows what's good for him," Joe's wife, Julie, instantly interjected from the seat beside him. "He might have something else wrapped around his neck at that point – and I'm not talking about his loving wife's arms either!" she continued rather quickly and quite convincingly.

"Exactly!" Chuck exclaimed knowingly. "So; how many times do those who truly love and want to please the Lord alone, have to be told by Him, precisely what type of worship music He wants before they decide to honor His wishes instead of their own? He has told us all very clearly, not once, not twice, not three, not even six, but a grand total of eight different times in the New Testament, exactly the type of worship music He wants in celebration to Him: singing – and singing only. [1] What makes us think, as feeble human beings, that we therefore have any authority [2] to give Him something else – something we might prefer or even see as better – over what He has so thoroughly indicated? Besides, folks need to remember that

Jesus said we show our love for Him by doing what He said, and not by doing what we might want instead." [3]

Completely caught off guard by the absolute simplicity of such sound, simple, and logical biblical reasoning, all Joe could stammer was, "But... what about David? He used instruments!"

"He also offered up animal sacrifices and danced uncovered before the Lord [4] too," Chuck said, chuckling, "but that doesn't mean that those Old Testament practices are a part of New Testament church worship. [5]

"It's like this... Let's go back to the pearls example. Suppose your first wife loved puzzles. She had a huge puzzle collection. Every holiday you sought to purchase her a new and unique puzzle. She eventually passes away and you remarry. Your new wife makes it extremely clear that she loves pearls – not puzzles. What would you get her when you want to celebrate her special day? Puzzles... or pearls?"

"If I'm the second wife, it better not be puzzles!" Joe's wife chillingly chimed in once again from her nearby lawn chair.

"Well, it's the same way with God. Under the Old Mosaic Covenant with the Israelites, sure, they used instruments. It was a very 'physically-oriented' system. However, under the New Covenant of Christ, [6] which is a much more 'spiritually-oriented' system, we see that God insists, not on some talented few playing their instruments in worship to Him while the rest look on, but on every single and grateful saint in the congregation **singing** His praises and putting their whole mind and spirit into it; teaching, admonishing, and encouraging one another while singing and making melody to the Lord with grateful hearts and cheerful lips! This is what the eight, exclusive New Testament messages or passages from God on the type of music He desires tell us. Our preacher posted quite an in-depth bible study on this to his website at: **www.Godswordistruth.org**. It's posted under "Bible Studies," and it's entitled ***Instrumental Music in Christian Worship and Gatherings Of Christ's New Testament Church Is a Direct Violation of the Word and Will of God*** [7] I think. If you really want to learn more about the music that God both desires and requires of His New Testament people, then you really ought to check it out and see what you think.

"And as far as who's right or wrong, Joe… we in the churches of Christ absolutely believe that the only way to be sure that a person is going to heaven, is to be as close to being right with God as they can possibly be. And that the only way they can do that, is simply to study everything out, "book, chapter, and verse," and then do everything exactly the way God said, period [8]. …Don't you, Joe? Well…don't you?"

ENDNOTES:

1.   **Matthew 26:30; Mark 14:26 (ESV):** And when they had sung a hymn, they went out to the Mount of Olives…

   Acts 16:25 (ESV): About midnight Paul and Silas were praying and singing hymns to God, and the prisoners were listening to them,

   Romans 15:9 (ESV): …and in order that the Gentiles might glorify God for his mercy. As it is written, "Therefore I will praise you among the Gentiles, and sing to your name."

   1ˢᵗ Corinthians 14:15 (ESV): What am I to do? I will pray with my spirit, but I will pray with my mind also; I will sing praise with my spirit, but I will sing with my mind also.

   Ephesians 5:19 (ESV): …addressing one another in psalms and hymns and spiritual songs, singing and making melody to the Lord with all your heart,

   Colossians 3:16 (ESV): Let the word of Christ dwell in you richly, teaching and admonishing one another in all wisdom, singing psalms and hymns and spiritual songs, with thankfulness in your hearts to God.

   Hebrews 2:12 (ESV): …saying, "I will tell of your name to my brothers; in the midst of the congregation I will sing your praise."

   James 5:13 (ESV): Is anyone among you suffering? Let him pray. Is anyone cheerful? Let him sing praise.

2.   **Matthew 28:18-20:** And Jesus came and spoke to them, saying, "All authority has been given to Me in heaven and on earth. Go therefore and make disciples of all the nations, baptizing them in the name of the Father and of the Son and of the Holy Spirit, teaching them to observe

all things that I have commanded you; and lo, I am with you always, *even* to the end of the age." Amen.

3. **John 14:15-23:** "If you love Me, keep My command-ments… He who has My commandments and keeps them, it is he who loves Me. And he who loves Me will be loved by My Father, and I will love him and manifest Myself to him. …If anyone loves Me, he will keep My word; and My Father will love him, and We will come to him and make Our home with him."

4. **2nd Samuel 6:13-20:** And it was so, that when they that bare the ark of the LORD had gone six paces, he sacrificed oxen and fatlings. And David danced before the LORD with all his might; and David was girded with a linen ephod. So David and all the house of Israel brought up the ark of the LORD with shouting, and with the sound of the trumpet. And as the ark of the LORD came into the city of David, Michal Saul's daughter looked through a window, and saw King David leaping and dancing before the LORD; and she despised him in her heart. And they brought in the ark of the LORD, and set it in his place, in the midst of the tabernacle that David had pitched for it: and David offered burnt offerings and peace offerings before the LORD. And as soon as David had made an end of offering burnt offerings and peace offerings, he blessed the people in the name of the LORD of hosts. And he dealt among all the people, even among the whole multitude of Israel, as well to the women as men, to every one a cake of bread, and a good piece of flesh, and a flagon of wine. So all the people departed every one to his house. Then David returned to bless his household. And Michal the daughter of Saul came out to meet David, and said, "How glorious was the king of Israel to day, who uncovered himself to day in the eyes of the handmaids of his servants, as one of the vain fellows shamelessly uncovereth himself!"

5. Please read and study **Hebrews, chapters 7 – 12** for further details.

6. **2ⁿᵈ Corinthians 3:5-8:** Not that we are sufficient of ourselves to think of anything as *being* from ourselves, but our sufficiency *is* from God, who also made us sufficient as ministers of the new covenant, not of the letter but of the Spirit; for the letter kills, but the Spirit gives life. But if the ministry of death, written *and* engraved on stones, was glorious, so that the children of Israel could not look steadily at the face of Moses because of the glory of his countenance, which *glory* was passing away, how will the ministry of the Spirit not be more glorious?

7. **Please see:** *"Worksheet Study - The Sin Of Offering Instrumental Music To God"* at **www.Godswordistruth.org**

8. **2ⁿᵈ Timothy 3:16-17:** All Scripture *is* given by inspiration of God, and *is* profitable for doctrine, for reproof, for correction, for instruction in righteousness, that the man of God may be complete, thoroughly equipped for every good work.

Chapter Three Questions for Classroom Discussion

1) Have you ever heard someone comment that the churches of Christ are the group that "doesn't have music?" How did you respond? How was your response different from Chuck's?

2) How many times does the Lord God have to tell us something before it is valid?

3) How many times total, did God clearly tell His New Testament people exactly the kind of music He wants – singing?

4) Can you recite those references on New Testament music, having committed them to memory so that you will be able to "give an answer," should you be called upon to do so?

5) Who is the only One who has the authority to command what type of music Christ's blood-bought church uses?

6) How does the bible state that we prove and confirm our love for Christ and the Father, in John 14:15-23? What is the connection between that passage and this modern-day parable involving Chuck and Joe?

7) Please read and explain/discuss how John 4:23-24 and Luke 6:46-49 fit into this chapter in their story as well.

8) Please explain a few of the differences between God's Old Covenant with the Israelites, and His New Covenant with Christians.

9) Please give at least three different references which prove we are no longer under the Old Covenant that allowed instrumental religious music.

10) Please read 1st Corinthians 10:1-13, and then explain what we can learn from those Old Testament examples, even though we are no longer under the Mosaic Covenant as law.

Chapter Four:

'Playing' With Fire

"I appreciate the ride home very much, Joe, thanks," Chuck said as both he and his co-worker climbed into Joe's car Thursday afternoon after work. "I didn't think my car would take two days at the garage."

"No problem, Chuck," Joe replied. "I've been wanting to talk with you anyway about something and this'll be a good chance to do that."

"What's on your mind, Joe?" Chuck asked cheerfully.

"It's about the whole instrumental music thing we discussed a little bit ago. Now I really appreciated the whole 'pearls and puzzles' illustration and everything - and I understood it very well. But really, what's the big deal about instrumental worship music anyway? None of the other churches I've ever tried seem to have a problem with it. And besides, I was just talking to my brother whose father-in-law is a Baptist preacher, and he said that the bible never says we can't use it, so why the fuss?" Joe blurted out all at once, wondering what Chuck's response would ultimately be. *After all*, he thought to himself, *if God had as big a problem with instrumental worship music as Chuck and the church of Christ seemed to think, then surely there should be some biblical reason... right?*

"He's exactly right, Joe," Chuck responded. "There is no New Testament verse anywhere, specifically stating that we are not to use instruments in our songs of praise and worship."

Joe smiled somewhat smugly. *Finally!* He thought.

"There doesn't have to be," Chuck continued, "and here's why. When God specifies for us exactly what He **does** want, He doesn't have to tell us all the things that that means He **doesn't** want. We see this in multiple passages throughout scripture. For example, in Leviticus 10:1-3,[1] God incinerated two of his own priests, Nadab and Abihu. Do you know what for, Joe?"

Joe shook his head no, wondering why he'd never heard a sermon about these two before in any of the several different denominations he and his family had previously visited

"For using fire on God's altar from a source other than that which He had specifically told them to," Chuck continued. "You see, God had told them very specifically where they were to get the fire He wanted them to place on His altar. And when He did, it automatically excluded all other sources. He didn't have to expressly tell them all the other places in the world where they were not to get fire from; when He told them where they were to get it, that excluded all others – at least for the faithful soul seeking to please God instead of themselves. And that's really what it boils down to Joe; it's a matter of obedient faith born of a complete trust in God.

"The same can be said for King David, the great 'man after God's own heart.' [2] God had given extremely specific instructions as to how He wanted His Ark of the Covenant moved; it was to be borne on the shoulders of the Levites. [3] David, however, had a different idea. Duplicating the precedent of those pagans who did not know God's specific instructions, [4] David tried to move the Ark using two milk cows and a new cart. God was so angry with David's lack of faith, obedience, and compliance with the way He said He wanted it moved, that when Uzzah the priest reached out to steady the Ark on the cart, God killed him as a sign of His divine displeasure. Why was God so angry? Remember: He had not specifically said His people **couldn't** use the cart and cows like the pagans who didn't know His Word had – but He didn't have to! When God had instructed that the Ark was to be borne on the shoulders of the Levites, then that automatically excluded all other options – without God having to list every single one! And remember; the reason for God's divine displeasure was because David didn't exhibit enough faith and loyalty to Him, to do it exactly the way God had commanded in His Word! [5]

"Remember, Jesus said, 'If you love Me, you'll obey My commandments.' [6] Hebrews 11 records many examples of the fact that in order to be pleasing to God, one must have faith enough in Him to **do** exactly **what** He said, exactly the **way** He said to do it. And I can show you eight different bible passages regarding the type of music God requires from His New

Testament, blood-bought children - and every single one of them says 'sing.' But neither you, your brother, your brother's preacher, nor any other person on the planet can show me one single New Testament verse where God commands His church to 'play' can they, Joe?"

Joe shook his head somewhat hesitantly.

"And when God says to 'sing,' He doesn't have to follow that up with, 'Now what I mean by that is, don't whistle, don't hum, don't play an instrument, don't whatever,'" Chuck continued. "Can you imagine how thick that would make our bibles? By stating specifically how He *does* want something done, God has successfully eliminated all other kinds of... well, 'fire' if you're Nadab and Abihu; 'Ark transportation' if you're David; or 'musical expression' if you're a New Testament Christian."

"And instrumental music is obviously a very different form of music from vocal or acappella," Joe said thoughtfully.

"Yes; and to show just how serious God is about this 'silence' - or not having to note all the exceptions when He gives specific instructions - consider that, according to Hebrews 7:13-14, even though God's message through Moses '*spoke nothing,*' or was completely silent concerning whether or not priests could come from the tribe of Judah, He didn't have to! When He said they must be from the tribe of Levi, that settled it by excluding priests coming from any of the other tribes automatically – even to the point that His perfect Son, Jesus Christ Himself could not have served as the one exception to His divine instruction," [7] Chuck said. "Take a good look at that passage when you get home tonight, Joe. It really proves the point. God doesn't have to tell us *not* to use instruments in order for it to be so. All He has to do is exactly what He did. And when He said 'sing,' eight times, that settled it."

"Wife called and asked me to stop and pick up a gallon of milk and a loaf of white bread," Joe interjected as he suddenly pulled into the local Hopeland grocery store. "And you're right; she didn't have to say, 'Now what I mean by that is don't buy eggs, bologna, paper towels, bottled water, or anything else. When she said, 'a gallon of milk and a loaf of bread,' that eliminated all those other things," Joe conceded. "I see what you mean. We use that logic everyday without even thinking about it – it's not just a bible thing is it?"

Chuck shook his head knowingly. "And it would be a 'big deal' if you instead brought home something other than what she specifically called to tell you to, wouldn't it Joe – such as a bottle of laxative and a bag of onions? How do you think she'd respond if you showed up with those instead? But because you love your wife, want to please her, and trust her to know what she wants, needs, and is talking about, you simply go in and get her what she wants without her having to state the dozens or even hundreds and thousands of other items in the store she doesn't want, don't you, Joe? So... why should it be any different with those that truly love the Lord when it comes to precisely what He wants us all to do in worship?

ENDNOTES:

1. **Leviticus 10:1-3 (ESV):** Now Nadab and Abihu, the sons of Aaron, each took his censer and put fire in it and laid incense on it and offered unauthorized fire before the LORD, which he had not commanded them. And fire came out from before the LORD and consumed them, and they died before the LORD. Then Moses said to Aaron, "This is what the LORD has said, 'Among those who are near me I will be sanctified, and before all the people I will be glorified.'"

2. **Acts 13:22:** He raised up for them David as king, to whom also He gave testimony and said, 'I have found David the son of Jesse, a man after My own heart, who will do all My will.'

3. **Deuteronomy 10:8:** At that time the LORD separated the tribe of Levi to bear the ark of the covenant of the LORD, to stand before the LORD to minister to Him and to bless in His name, to this day.

4. **Please see: 1ˢᵗ Samuel 6:1-13.**

5. **Please see 1ˢᵗ Chronicles, chapters 13 & 15** for complete details.

6. **John 14:15:** "If you Love Me, keep My commandments."

7. **Hebrews 7:13-14:** For He of whom these things are spoken belongs to another tribe, from which no man has officiated at the altar. For *it is* evident that our Lord arose from Judah, of which tribe Moses spoke nothing concerning priesthood.

Chapter Four Questions for Classroom Discussion

1) Where is the New Testament verse which specifically forbids the use of instrumental praise music for the Lord's New Testament church?

2) When God says exactly what He does want, what does that say exactly, about what He doesn't want?

3) What kind of fire does the bible call the kind Nadab and Abihu used? Had God specifically said don't use it?

4) Where did David get his original idea for moving the Ark of the Covenant? What happened when he did it that way?

5) Where did David then get the idea to use the Levites instead (See 1st Chronicles 15:11-15)? What happened when he did it that way?

6) Giving God exactly what He said He wanted by doing things exactly as He specified, is called something in Hebrews 11. What is it?

7) What does the bible say about priests from the tribe of Judah, according to Hebrews 7:13-14?

   Just because the bible said nothing about priests from there – just as the New Testament is silent when it comes to condemning the use of instrumental music in the church's worship – did that mean a priest from a tribe other than the tribe of Judah which God had specified would still be okay with Him? What about if that priest were even His perfect Son?

8) If God almighty would not allow His own perfect Son, Jesus Christ Himself, to be an exception to His rule, that when He specifies a certain type of thing that that eliminates all other types, then why do some people seem to think that they have more authority than Jesus, or that

God will somehow make exceptions for their desires when it comes to the unauthorized use of their mechanical instruments of music in New Testament worship?

9) Discuss several everyday examples of instances where we all use this same simple reasoning, that when someone asks us to perform a specific task, or take a specific action, that eliminates all the other thousands of possibilities we could have done. Apply this to the type of music God has specified.

10) Does there have to be a specific verse wherein God has to state that we are not to use instruments in the music we give Him, in order for that to be binding and expected of the faithful?

11) Does the term "determined disobedience" enter into the instrumental music issue as we have studied it? Does this make it a "big deal" to God?

NOTES

Chapter Five:

Baptism Essential?
That's Just Your Interpretation!

"But that's just your interpretation; yours and the rest of those folks up at the church of Christ where you go," Joe said as he and his co-worker Chuck discussed the bible during their lunch break. "Baptism actually has nothing to do with initially getting saved – it comes after! Everybody knows that!"

Chuck slowly looked around at their co-workers at the other picnic tables enjoying the noon hour sunshine. As his eyes settled on Simon who sat engrossed in the local paper, he thoughtfully turned back to Joe and said, "Let me ask you a question, Joe. Suppose in today's paper, there was a Hopeland Store ad that read, 'Free, fifty-dollar Hopeland gift cards given out to the first fifty families to come through the door this coming Friday. Gift cards valid at local location only, and expire Friday night at midnight. One card per family; must be eighteen or older to obtain card.'"

"Now, what if someone showed up Thursday evening, was sixteen, and wanted a card? Would they get one?" Chuck asked.

Joe shook his head no.

"Well, what about if a person showed up Friday morning, stood in line, and was a member of the fifty-third family to enter the store? Should they expect one?"

Again, Joe shook his head no.

"Or, try this," Chuck continued. "What if someone showed up, was over eighteen, was part of the sixth family to enter the store on Friday morning, received their card, and then either tried to cash it in on Saturday, or over at Mall-Mart, or at the Land Springs Hopeland Store thirty miles from here - even if a friend or family member that they totally trusted had told them that that's what the rules actually meant, despite what they literally said in big, bold, black and white print in today's paper?"

Joe, beginning to get just a little bit frustrated at Chuck's seemingly endless and somewhat elementary inquiries, responded rather impatiently, "Well then, no, of course they wouldn't get to spend the card. Look Chuck, I can read. What's your point?"

"The point is simply this, Joe," Chuck answered patiently. "And it's an extremely important one. How is it that the whole town can - and is completely expected to without a single second thought - read and understand an ad like I've described, exactly alike? One reading, and they completely understand and accept the implications of every aspect of the ad, and then plan and act accordingly? They understand the "ground rules" of receiving this free gift card, without exception, exemption, or interpretation. They read and immediately accept that the rules mean exactly what they say, as written in straightforward black and white, and prepare to meet the requirements if they want to receive the free gift. ...And yet, when it comes to some of the bible's plainest, simplest, most straightforward, and easiest to understand of instructions, some of those very same folks seem to always want to insist that those are somehow a 'matter of interpretation' and that it's therefore okay if we all understand them completely differently." [1]

Chuck leaned in very seriously and stared Joe straight in the eye. "Joe, you don't believe that man is smarter than God, do you? I know you don't. And yet, if anyone believes that a salesman-authored ad and its written requirements to receive a free gift can be easily understood alike by all who read it, but that somehow God's straightforward black and white written requirements in order to receive His free gift cannot be, then what they are actually saying is that a mere human being is smart enough to know how to communicate clearly with men, while their almighty God and all-knowing Creator is somehow not. Think about that for a minute Joe..."

"And, let me give you an example," Chuck said as he thumbed through the well-worn pages of the small bible he always kept handy at work. "Please read this passage," he said as he handed Joe his bible, pointing to Mark 16:15-16.

"And He said to them, 'Go into all the world and preach the gospel to every creature. He who believes and is baptized will be saved; but he who does not believe will be condemned,'" Joe read slowly aloud.

"Now," Chuck continued, "a simple question; honestly, how do you 'interpret' that particular verse Joe? Does it mean that he who believes is saved at that point, and should sometime thereafter be baptized as so many teach today? Or does it mean exactly what it says – that belief and baptism both precede being saved?"

Joe's mind raced to find a reasonable response. He could read and he knew he was caught. His indefensible and flimsy fog of man-made excuses and explanations were being blown away by the blinding light of God's Word right before his very eyes. [2] It was also at that moment that something else occurred to him for the very first time as well. The way that verse read, if he said that baptism wasn't essential to and must precede being saved, then the same could be said for the other element that verse contained – that belief wasn't essential to and must precede being saved either – and he knew better than to say that... and so, he said nothing instead. [3]

Sitting there in the suddenly stifling silence and sensing his friend's indecision, Chuck softly tried again. "When we read in Acts 2:38, that Peter answered those seeking God's forgiveness by saying that they should 'Repent and be baptized, every one of them in the name of Jesus for the forgiveness of sins,' what did he literally mean? Really, how would you 'interpret' that Joe? That they should say a prayer inviting Jesus into their hearts to be forgiven and then should be baptized? That baptism was nothing more than an outward sign of an inward grace, and as an indication that salvation had already occurred sometime previously? Or... that they needed to be baptized specifically FOR the forgiveness of their sins, just as it very simply and plainly says in straightforward black and white?" [4]

"But... we're saved by faith and faith alone!" Joe justified... "Baptism doesn't save anyone!" Joe continued without much conviction, resorting only to quoting what he'd heard so many denominational preachers so proudly spout so many times before...

"Okay; let's assume for a moment that you're right Joe... Then... what do you make of this?" Chuck asked as he thumbed through to the book of James, then pointing Joe to James 2:19-24 [5] and asking him to read it. Phrases like 'even the demons believe - and shudder,' and, 'You see then that a man is justified by works, and NOT by faith only' struck and stuck in Joe's mind as if delivered by a divine and undeniable spiritual sledgehammer.

"You see," Chuck continued, "baptism specifically for the forgiveness or washing away of our sins is how and when we call on the name of the Lord to be saved, according to Acts 22:16. [6] It is the also the act of faith by which we become God's children, according to Galatians 3:26-27. [7] Let's take a look at those two texts and see if it's even possible that yours or anyone else's 'interpretation' wouldn't be exactly the same as -"

Just then the whistle signaling the end of their lunch hour suddenly sounded. Hastily gathering up their lunch containers and disposing of their garbage, Chuck, quite concerned for his friend's soul, chimed in one more time, "Listen Joe, if anyone truly believes that baptism doesn't have anything to do with saving us - especially when 1st Peter 3:21 expressly states that 'baptism DOES now save us' [8] – well, that's not a matter of **interpretation**, but *interpolation*![9] If you truly believe the bible is God's Word, then let's get together and take a closer look at some of those texts tonight and what they really say, shall we? What do you say, Joe?"

ENDNOTES:

1. **2nd Peter 1:19-21:** And so we have the prophetic word confirmed, which you do well to heed as a light that shines in a dark place, until the day dawns and the morning star rises in your hearts; knowing this first, that no prophecy of Scripture is of any private interpretation, for prophecy never came by the will of man, but holy men of God spoke *as they were* moved by the Holy Spirit.

2. **2nd Corinthians 10:3-6:** For though we walk in the flesh, we do not war according to the flesh. For the weapons of our warfare *are* not carnal but mighty in God for pulling down strongholds, casting down arguments and every high thing that exalts itself against the knowledge of God, bringing every thought into captivity to the obedience of Christ, and being ready to punish all disobedience when your obedience is fulfilled.

3. **Mark 11:30-33:** "The baptism of John—was it from heaven or from men? Answer Me." And they reasoned among themselves, saying, "If we say, 'From heaven,' He will say, 'Why then did you not believe him?' But if we say, 'From men'"—they feared the people, for all counted John to have been a prophet indeed. So they answered and said to Jesus, "We do not know."

4. **Acts 2:38:** Then Peter said to them, "Repent, and let every one of you be baptized in the name of Jesus Christ for the remission of sins; and you shall receive the gift of the Holy Spirit."

5. **James 2:19-24:** You believe that there is one God. You do well. Even the demons believe—and tremble! But do you want to know, O foolish man, that faith without works is dead? Was not Abraham our father justified by works when he offered Isaac his son on the altar? Do you see that faith was working together with his works, and by

works faith was made perfect? And the Scripture was fulfilled which says, "Abraham believed

6. God, and it was accounted to him for righteousness." And he was called the friend of God. You see then that a man is justified by works, and not by faith only.

7. **Acts 22:16:** And now why are you waiting? Arise and be baptized, and wash away your sins, calling on the name of the Lord.

8. **Galatians 3:26-27:** For you are all sons of God through faith in Christ Jesus. For as many of you as were baptized into Christ have put on Christ.

9. **1ˢᵗ Peter 3:21 (ESV):** Baptism, which corresponds to this, now saves you, not as a removal of dirt from the body but as an appeal to God for a good conscience, through the resurrection of Jesus Christ.

ALSO PLEASE NOTE Colossians 2:8-13, in connection with the fact that baptism is not a 'work,' but **the** "act of faith" by which we access God's grace and forgiveness, and subsequently salvation: Beware lest anyone cheat you through philosophy and empty deceit, according to the tradition of men, according to the basic principles of the world, and not according to Christ. For in Him dwells all the fullness of the Godhead bodily; and you are complete in Him, who is the head of all principality and power. In Him you were also circumcised with the circumcision made without hands, by putting off the body of the sins of the flesh, by the circumcision of Christ, buried with Him in baptism, in which you also were raised with *Him* through faith in the working of God, who raised Him from the dead. And you, being dead in your trespasses and the uncircumcision of your flesh, He has made alive together with Him, having forgiven you all trespasses…

10. "Interpolate… 1) to alter, enlarge, or corrupt (a book or manuscript, etc.) by putting in new words, subject matter, etc. 2) to insert between or among others, specif., to insert (a word or words) in a text…" ~Webster's New World™ College Dictionary, Fourth Edition, © 1999 by MacMillan, USA.

Chapter Five Questions for Classroom Discussion

1) How many times in a day do you suppose, between newspaper and internet advertisements, television commercials, speed limit and traffic law signs, legal documents, product directions, school and college studies, workplace "Standard Operating Procedure" sheets, and all other written correspondence that you can possibly think of, are we all automatically expected to read and come to the exact same conclusion about?

2) And even if something does need a little explanation, clarification, or interpretation because of man's mis-communication (such as the sign I recently read while going by a convenience store which stated, "Ethanol Free Gas." Does that mean I can buy ethanol there as well as getting free gas to boot? Of course not!), doesn't a little common sense and objectivity go quite a long way?

3) Why do you think otherwise perfectly competent and completely functional, literate people so often fall back to the old "That's just your interpretation" line, when confronted by certain black and white biblical truths?

4) Please read/study the following passages: Romans 12:16, 15:5-6; 1st Corinthians 1:10; 2nd Corinthians 13:11; Philippians 1:27-2:2, 4:2; and 1st Peter 3:8. Please describe/discuss what these verses all have in common, and then relate that theme to the phrase, "It's all a matter of interpretation."

5) What are some of the implications of James 2:19-24 for those who believe one can be saved by "faith only?" Why do you think those who claim to believe that we are saved by faith **only**, then always insist that we must additionally say a prayer in order to be saved?

6) How/when exactly, does one biblically "call on the name of the Lord" to be saved, according to Acts 2:38 and 22:16? What does that do to the denominational 'interpretation' that Romans 10:9-13 is talking about saying a prayer instead?

7) What do Galatians 3:26-27 and Colossians 2:8-13 define baptism as; a 'work,' or an act of faith in God?

8) Look up and memorize the meaning of the term, "interpolation." What does it actually, literally mean?

9) How many words – and which word in particular – did Satan insert into God's instructions between Genesis 2:17 and 3:4? What word was it? How many words, and which one in particular, do people insert into God's instructions for salvation in 1st Peter 3:21, who say that "baptism does NOT now save you?" Where do you suppose that ploy comes from? Is it "interpretation," or "interpolation?" Explain.

Now, who else do you need to go explain that to?

NOTES

Chapter Six:

Enough to Raise the Dead!

What a different bunch these church of Christ folks are, Joe thought as he and his family filed silently out after the funeral service. A distant neighbor of theirs had died somewhat suddenly and the funeral service had been held at the church of Christ building due to the deceased's family request. Unfortunately, this funeral marked the first time that Joe and his family had been in the church of Christ's building, and he wasn't all that comfortable with it. Oh, he liked the members there well enough; they all seemed very loving and sincere. He particularly liked his church of Christ co-worker, Chuck Churchman, and his family; they never seemed to be at a loss for a simple and straightforward biblical answer to any question he had. [1] Thanks to them, he now even understood the biblical reasons why these folks didn't use instruments in their worship to God, [2] and he was even beginning to understand the biblical reasons they insisted that baptism was essential to salvation. [3] These weren't matters of opinion, personal preference, or even interpretation, but of simply and faithfully following God's New Testament biblical pattern. [4] How could that possibly be wrong? In fact, how could anything other than that possibly be right in the eyes of God?

No, what troubled him today was that he had attended this funeral, and no one had even spoken in tongues! Wasn't tongue-speaking a sign of Holy-Spirit anointing and of one's eternal salvation? That's what the T.V. preacher he used to listen to so often said. He would have to ask Chuck about that, and soon...

The next morning as he drove into the parking lot, he saw Chuck arriving at the same time. Chuck waved Joe into the empty parking space nearest the building and parked his own car further away, down near the back end of the lot. Joe waited for Chuck to walk up.

"Good morning Joe; glad to see you at Bill's funeral yesterday," Chuck said. "Everything okay? You seemed a little down."

"Not down, just a little confused," Joe countered.

"About what?" Chuck inquired.

"Well… yesterday… to be honest, at the service… Where it was a funeral and everything, I expected that certainly someone there – the preacher, one of the song leaders or someone - would surely speak in tongues! I mean, after all, shouldn't a group of people claiming to be Christ's be publicly able to prove the power of the Holy Ghost's acceptance of them by their speaking in tongues?"

Chuck grinned knowingly, and politely said, "That'll teach you to watch and take to heart everything those T.V. preachers and false teachers say who want to tickle people's ears so they can steal 'em blind, won't it?" [5]

Joe shrugged.

"You see, Joe, the Bible explains in Mark 16:17-20, that the possession of the "miraculous gifts" was given to confirm that the Word the apostles brought was indeed from God; these gifts were given to get people's attention just as they did indeed do in Acts 2, so people would then listen to the apostles' preaching. And, you might also notice as you read down through Acts 2:1-11, that these 'tongues' were not the unknown, gibberish-typed gobbledygook that you hear false teachers claim as legitimate tongue-speaking today, oh no. They were actually, instead, very recognizable, instantaneously-spoken, and perfectly dialected and well-known languages! That chapter also shows us in verse 43 that only the apostles – and then those whom the apostles would lay their hands on thereafter as we see in Acts 6:5-6 with 8:5-18 – possessed those gifts.

Later on, Cornelius and his household also received them in Acts 10, but that was a one-time thing to prove that the Gentiles were now included and accepted under the New Covenant, as Peter went on to thereafter explain in Acts 11:1-18. The Bible is clear in 1st Corinthians though, that when the entire New Testament was finally revealed and written down by around 100 A.D., that the miraculous gifts would cease, because they would have fulfilled their original purpose and would no longer be needed to confirm the Word of God which the apostles brought."

"But here's the simpler, common-sense bottom line if you'd prefer," Chuck continued. "There are many so-called 'charismatic' denominations or divisions around today, which claim that the 'miraculous gifts' of speaking in tongues, healing the sick, casting out demons, and raising the dead are still in effect, correct?"

"Well, I don't know about raising the dead," Joe replied.

"Oh yes; you can't pick and choose," Chuck said. "With God, it's all or nothing. Jesus and His first-century apostles possessed the power to raise the dead just as surely as they did to heal the sick - just as several scriptures verify for us [6] - and just as these churches claim they can do today."

"Actually," Joe responded a bit sheepishly, "I know they do. My wife grew up in one; her parents were extremely strong members."

"Oh really? Didn't know that. Where are they now?" Chuck humbly asked.

"Her dad is dead, and her mom is in a nursing home suffering from Alzh--------." Suddenly, the simple, scriptural, and all-illuminating truth of God's Word struck him like a bolt of lightning!

"Exactly," Chuck said sadly, noting the light of understanding now piercing his friend's understanding. "I realize that there are many sincere and well-intentioned people in most of these man-made and named churches. But if some of them actually **possessed,** half of the miraculous gifts they **professed**, then why do their own members still get sick and die? Why do they and their preachers still have health insurance? Where's their faith to practice what they preach? Why do they ever have to have a funeral service held in their buildings? How come they haven't raised some of their own deceased leaders from the dead if they can truly do what they claim they can? In fact, how come they got sick and died in the first place if they possessed the gift of healing? And; why don't they go out onto the front lines of our armed forces and raise our brave and fallen soldiers as soon as they're killed so they can fight on? Why don't they go to our big city hospitals daily and heal the sick and dying little children in those cancer wards

- if they really can? How can they claim to love others, and to possess those gifts, and then not exercise them to the glory of God in this sick and pain-filled existence? I don't mean to be mean or harsh, but just simply honest. And I'm not judging, I'm simply asking. And please don't insult us both by giving me that, 'the afflicted didn't have enough faith' stuff. I doubt that any of the dead that Jesus, Peter, or Paul raised from the dead had much faith at that point either." [6]

Joe, now momentarily silenced – even stupefied - by the sheer simplicity of that which he had never even in reality considered before, just stood there, somewhat stunned… "Is there any way you can biblically prove, 'book, chapter, and verse,' as you say, what you've just said?" Joe humbly and awkwardly asked.

"Sure," Chuck replied, sensing and seeking to help heal the hurt and helplessness his uninformed friend was now struggling with. "Go home tonight and download *The Miraculous Gifts of the Holy Spirit; Are They Still in Effect Today as Some Claim?*[7] from our church's website at **www.Godswordistruth.org**, and then let's get together over an open bible and talk about it, okay Joe?"

ENDNOTES:

1. **John 8:31-32:** Then Jesus said to those Jews who believed Him, "If you abide in My word, you are My disciples indeed. And you shall know the truth, and the truth shall make you free."

    John 12:48-50: He who rejects Me, and does not receive My words, has that which judges him--the word that I have spoken will judge him in the last day. For I have not spoken on My own *authority;* but the Father who sent Me gave Me a command, what I should say and what I should speak. And I know that His command is everlasting life. Therefore, whatever I speak, just as the Father has told Me, so I speak."

    John 14:21-24 (Excerpted): He who has My commandments and keeps them, it is he who loves Me. And he who loves Me will be loved by My Father, and I will love him and manifest Myself to him." ... "If anyone loves Me, he will keep My word; and My Father will love him, and We will come to him and make Our home with him. He who does not love Me does not keep My words; and the word which you hear is not Mine but the Father's who sent Me."

    John 17:17: "Sanctify them by Your truth. Your word is truth."

    2ⁿᵈ Timothy 3:15-17: And that from childhood you have known the Holy Scriptures, which are able to make you wise for salvation through faith which is in Christ Jesus. All Scripture *is* given by inspiration of God, and *is* profitable for doctrine, for reproof, for correction, for instruction in righteousness, that the man of God may be complete, thoroughly equipped for every good work (2ⁿᵈ Timothy 3:15-17).

2nd Peter 1:20-21: Knowing this first, that no prophecy of Scripture is of any private interpretation, for prophecy never came by the will of man, but holy men of God spoke *as they were* moved by the Holy Spirit.

2.　**Please see:** "*Worksheet Study - The Sin Of Offering Instrumental Music To God*" at **www.Godswordistruth.org**

3.　**1st Peter 3:21 (ESV):** Baptism, which corresponds to this, now saves you, not as a removal of dirt from the body but as an appeal to God for a good conscience, through the resurrection of Jesus Christ.

4.　**2nd Timothy 1:13:** Hold fast the pattern of sound words which you have heard from me, in faith and love which are in Christ Jesus.

5.　**2nd Timothy 4:1-5:** I charge *you* therefore before God and the Lord Jesus Christ, who will judge the living and the dead at His appearing and His kingdom: Preach the word! Be ready in season *and* out of season. Convince, rebuke, exhort, with all longsuffering and teaching. For the time will come when they will not endure sound doctrine, but according to their own desires, *because* they have itching ears, they will heap up for themselves teachers; and they will turn *their* ears away from the truth, and be turned aside to fables. But you be watchful in all things, endure afflictions, do the work of an evangelist, fulfill your ministry.

2nd Peter 2:1-3: But there were also false prophets among the people, even as there will be false teachers among you, who will secretly bring in destructive heresies, even denying the Lord who bought them, *and* bring on themselves swift destruction. And many will follow their destructive ways, because of whom the way of truth will be blasphemed. By covetousness they will exploit you with deceptive words; for a long time their judgment has not been idle, and their destruction does not slumber.

6. <u>**Please see and study: Matthew 10:7-8; Mark 5:35-42;**</u>
    <u>**Luke 7:11-32; John 5:21-29, 11:1-44, 12:1-18; Acts**</u>
    <u>**9:36-41, 20:7-12, and 19:11-20...**</u>

7. **Please see:** *"The Miraculous Gifts Of The Holy Spirit"*
    Bible Study at **www.Godswordistruth.org**

Chapter Six Questions for Classroom Discussion

1) Is there really a pattern we are to follow according to the Apostle Paul?

2) Please review 2nd Peter 2:1-3... What does the bible say about the purpose behind those who proclaim false doctrines today, such as the notion that the miraculous gifts are still in effect which they cannot legitimately perform?

3) Please review 2nd Thessalonians 2:9-12... Who did Paul say was also capable of signs and wonders?

4) Please review Mark 16:15-20... Why were the miraculous gifts originally given?

   According to Acts 1:1-8, to whom was the promise of the miraculous gifts given?

   According to Acts 2:1-4 and 43, to whom were the miraculous gifts given?

   According to Acts 8:17-18, how were the miraculous gifts passed along?

   (So, what happened to that ability when the last apostle passed away?)

   According to Acts 11:1-18, what was the purpose of God's giving the miraculous gifts to Cornelius and his household?

   According to 1st Corinthians 13:8-13, when would the end of the miraculous gifts come?

   For further explanation/insight/understanding on the above, please see: "*The Miraculous Gifts Of The Holy Spirit*" Bible Study at **www.Godswordistruth.org**.

5) Please make a list of all the different, legitimate, recognizable and instantaneously exhibited foreign languages and dialects (this is what the miraculous 'speaking in tongues' in the bible always consisted of) represented in Acts 2:4-12. How many did you count?

6) Did those disciples in the bible who could speak in tongues and heal the sick have any problems raising the dead just as easily? What does this say for those who would like us to believe today that they can legitimately speak in tongues and heal the sick?

7) Please prepare to answer/discuss the following questions straight out of the conversation itself:

Why do those preachers who proclaim that the gifts of healing are still here today still have health insurance? Where's their faith to practice what they preach? Why do they ever have to have funeral services held in their buildings if they can really raise the dead as Jesus and His apostles did? How come they haven't raised their leaders like Oral Roberts from the dead if they can truly do what they claim they can? Why don't they go out onto the front lines of our armed forces and raise the fallen as soon as they're killed so they can fight on? Why don't they travel to city hospital wards daily and heal the sick and dying little children in those cancer wards - if they really can? How can they claim to love, and to have those gifts, and then not exercise them to the glory of God in this sick and pain-filled existence?

NOTES

Chapter Seven:

Grate Feelings; Grilled Souls

"Thanks so much for having us over for dinner," Joe said, as He and Chuck stood and enjoyed the backyard aroma of barbecuing beef mingling with the smell of fresh-cut grass slowly wafting its way off into the early evening breeze.

"No problem," Chuck said with the same joviality he usually displayed as he once again flipped the meat, "glad to have you."

"And I really appreciate all the invitations to church and the bible studies and everything too, but I just really believe and feel in my heart that I'm saved. After all, I don't cheat on my taxes or beat my wife – I'm actually not that bad of a guy, considering…" Joe slightly smiled as he somewhat humbly stated.

"Oh, I think you're a great guy too, Joe – no doubt about it," Chuck quickly responded. "'Love your whole family; so glad we all got to know each other. But the question is, is someone's simply being a 'good person' really enough to get one into heaven - according to God? If you believe it is, then how do you 'interpret' John 14:6 wherein Jesus said, "I am the way, the truth, and the life. No one comes to the Father except through Me?'"

Joe paused. He and Chuck had already had the 'interpretation' versus 'interpolation' discussion. And he had actually gone home and looked up the definition of the latter, and it meant something like 'to alter or corrupt a book or manuscript by inserting new words into a text.' He certainly did not want to do that here like he had foolishly done during their 1st Peter 3:21 discussion about baptism, wherein he had subconsciously added the word 'not' to 'baptism does now save you,' not at all dissimilar to what the devil had done in the garden…

"And as to your feeling in your heart that you're already saved, let me ask you a very serious question Joe," Chuck continued, as he put down the tongs and closed the grill cover. "Let's suppose your wife has been having some very painful headaches of late. You go to the doctors and they perform a whole bunch of tests. A week later, the doctor has you return to discuss the test results. As you sit down, he somberly says, 'I'm afraid I have some tragic news. Test results have repeatedly validated that Julie has an inoperable brain tumor; its size and location typically indicate very little time left.' How do you feel when you hear that Joe?"

Joe swallowed hard and tried to internalize the unimaginable pain and anguish such a devastating diagnosis would bring – all of the sudden wanting to step inside where Julie was helping Charlotte prepare a salad and hug his wife.

"And what about the ride home and the feeling around your house that evening? Can you imagine the terribly painful thoughts, and feelings of fear and inadequacy - not to mention the torrential tears – that you'd all be experiencing at that point?"

"Not really," Joe said hesitantly. "That would be the most awful thing I could ever imagine."

"Not to be insensitive my friend, but would those feelings be real?" Chuck asked.

Joe's eyes flashed as he quickly retorted, "Of course they would!"

"I know they would. Now consider this," Chuck quietly continued, sorry that he had had to put his friend in such a tragic state of mind in order to hopefully help him to perhaps better understand the truth. "What if the next morning, the doctor's office called and said that they'd made a terrible mistake; that the test results they'd discussed with you weren't really your wife's at all but a 'Mrs. Clavenders' instead of a 'Mrs. Clevelanders?'"

"I'd sue the snot out of them – I'd own that office!" Joe blurted out violently.

"But my question is this Joe," Chuck said, slowly allowing his point to sink in. "Would your heart-felt feelings, the afternoon before, have been any less real or painful at the time, just because they were innocently and unknowingly based on totally false information?

"No, I don't suppose they would," Joe answered.

"And this is exactly why the bible so clearly and consistently illustrates why we must not allow our feelings to overshadow our faith and trust in exactly what the Word of God says; because so often those feelings - despite their great strength and intensity at the time – may be based solely on completely false information. For instance, do you remember the story of Adam and Eve? [1] She understood what God had said. But she later chose to believe the false information Satan gave her, and apparently felt it would be okay to eat from the tree. Do you remember where that got her?" Chuck asked.

"Kicked out of paradise and away from the presence of God?" Joe responded.

"Exactly," Chuck said. "And then there's the story of Jacob in Genesis 37. His sons sold their younger brother Joseph into slavery and convinced their dad Jacob that he had been killed by wild animals, showing him Joseph's bloodstained jacket as proof. But what they didn't tell Jacob was that they had sold their brother into slavery and dipped his coat in animal blood in order to falsely convince their father that his favorite son was dead. And Jacob was heartbroken! He was devastated! He felt dead inside himself! But even though his feelings were as absolutely real as could be, the 'evidence' on which they were based was totally false! [2]

"In 1st Samuel 10:8, King Saul was clearly told to go and wait for the prophet Samuel to come and offer the sacrifice at Gilgal. However, in 1st Samuel 13:1-14 we see that instead of acting in faith, he allowed his impatience to over-rule his obedience and offered the sacrifice himself. His excuse? His feelings; because he "felt compelled" it says in verse 12. And do you know what God called his going by his feelings instead of by faith in God's commandments in verse 13? Foolish.

"Additionally, the Lord taught His disciples that there would be those who would want to kill them, wrongly feeling that they would be offering service to God by so doing. [3] Those who had the Lord crucified felt that that was precisely what God wanted them to do as well. [4] Add to that Saul of Tarsus. Many years after his conversion to Christ, he confessed that in his earlier days he had felt so strongly that Christianity had to be exterminated that he was willing to kill to help expedite it [5] – sort of like the twin towers terrorists in 2001. In all of those cases, those people, like you, felt so completely convinced of certain things in their hearts [6] that some of them were even willing to go so far as to kill for their convictions. That's how strongly they 'believed in their hearts!' But every single one of them was wrong, Joe – dead wrong.

"But perhaps the scariest section of scripture showing the fact that feelings – no matter how sincere – can be so scathingly wrong as to cost countless millions their eternal souls, is found in Matthew 7:21-23. Those "many" people Jesus described therein had apparently believed with every fiber of their heart, soul, mind, and strength that they were saved – but their feelings had deceived them; they were most definitely not. [7] The fact is Joe, that how we feel or what anyone may have convinced themselves of, is not the standard of acceptance any of us are going to be judged on Judgment Day, but only and exclusively by the Word of God according to Jesus in John 12:48."

As Chuck turned to reopen the grill and turn the meat for the final time, Joe thoughtfully watched the smoke rise from the fiery pit of coals beneath, and suddenly understood in his heart for the very first time, that he dared not trust something as all-important as his soul's eternity, to just the fickleness of his heart-felt feelings. [8]

ENDNOTES:

1. **Please see: Genesis 2:15-3:24.**

2. **Please see: Genesis 37:1-35.**

3. **John 16:2:** They will put you out of the synagogues; yes, the time is coming that whoever kills you will think that He offers God service.

4. **John 11:47-53:** Then the chief priests and the Pharisees gathered a council and said, "What shall we do? For this Man works many signs. If we let Him alone like this, everyone will believe in Him, and the Romans will come and take way both our place and nation." And one of them, Caiaphas, being high priest that year, said to them, "You know nothing at all, nor do you consider that it is expedient for us that one man should die for the people, and not that the whole nation should perish." Now this he did not say on his own authority; but being high priest that year he prophesied that Jesus would die for the nation, and not for that nation only, but also that He would gather together in one the children of God who were scattered abroad. Then, from that day on, they plotted to put Him to death.

5. **Acts 26:9-11:** Indeed, I myself thought I must do many things contrary to the name of Jesus of Nazareth. This I also did in Jerusalem, and many of the saints I shut up in prison, having received authority from the chief priests; and when they were put to death, I cast my vote against them. And I punished them often in every synagogue and compelled them to blaspheme; and being exceedingly enraged against them, I persecuted them even to foreign cities.

6. **Jeremiah 17:9:** The heart is deceitful above all things, and desperately wicked; who can know it?

7. **Matthew 7:21-23:** Not everyone who says to Me, "Lord, Lord," shall enter the kingdom of heaven, but he who does the will of My Father who is in heaven. Many will say to Me in that day, "Lord, Lord, have we not prophesied in Your name, cast out demons in Your name, and done may wonders in Your name?" And then I will declare to them, "I never knew you; depart from Me, you who practice lawlessness!

8. **Proverbs 14:12 and 16:25:** There is a way that seems right to a man, but its end is the way of death.

Chapter Seven Questions for Classroom Discussion

1) Discuss how difficult it can be, dealing with seeking to convert to Jesus, someone who "just feels in [their] heart" that they're already saved.

2) What is the difference between the intensity level of a person's feelings that are based on what they believe and accept to be true at the time (even if unknown to them it isn't), and the intensity level of a person's feelings that are based on true information?

   Why is this so dangerous as we discuss the topic at hand?

   How do we need to seek to deal with such a situation?

3) Discuss what each of the following people felt was the right thing to do as outlined above; what they actually did because of their feelings; and where it got them...

   -Eve

   -Jacob

   -Those who would seek to kill the disciples

   -Those who sought and were successful in killing Jesus

   -Saul of Tarsus

   -The Twin Towers Terrorists in 2001

   -The religiously active, devoted, convicted and conscientious – but completely deceived and deluded of Matthew 7:21-23

4) Which of the above characters and their stories do you think would be the most effective in "cutting to the heart"

and converting those who "just believe in their heart" that they're saved? State and explain your choice.

5)   As to the "fickleness of one's feelings," do you believe it might also be a good illustration to remember as you seek to convert those whose "salvation" is based purely on their emotions, to note the difference in the multitude's reaction to Jesus in just the five short days between the Sunday afternoon He entered the Holy City like a conqueror, and the following Friday morning when He was led back outside its gates to be crucified like a common criminal (Matthew 21:7-11 and 27:20-43)? Why or why not?

Chapter Eight:

Fast Food Follies and Foolishness

"Great question, Joe; and one I'll be happy to answer in just a minute," Chuck said as the smiling Drive Thru server slid open the window and handed him their morning 'breakfast in a bag.' After sifting through and sorting out the contents and then slipping into an empty parking space and saying a sincere prayer of thanks for the day and the food, Chuck slowly pulled the car back out into the Saturday morning traffic as they continued on their way to the quarterly corporate safety meeting.

"My wife has been doing some fascinating research for an online financial and advertising business course she's taking," Chuck continued around bites of breakfast and sips of coffee. "Did you know that Burger King, Sonic, and Carl's Jr. are all actually just simply subsidiaries of the McDonalds Corporation?"

Joe turned and stared incredulously at Chuck, almost losing a bite of his breakfast from his now slack jaw in the process. "What on earth are you talking about?" he blurted out.

"Well," Chuck continued, "Charlotte's research revealed that McDonalds was the original fast-food burger joint. It was started in 1937, on route 66 in Monrovia, California, by a man named Patrick McDonald. His two sons later relocated it and changed the menu; Ray Kroc later purchased the rights to it and the rest is history. Today, their corporate headquarters is located in Oak Brook, Illinois.

"Then, based on the immense success of the McDonald's brothers' restaurant concept which had begun in earnest in California by 1948, five years later, in 1953, in Jacksonville, Florida, Keith Kramer and Matthew Burns founded a fledgling new copycat company hoping to mimic the McDonalds brothers' success, which eventually became 'Burger King.'

Their corporate headquarters is now located in Miami-Dade County, Florida.

"Carl's Jr. on the other hand, was started by a man named Carl Karcher in 1941, when he and his wife Margaret borrowed $311 (using their car as collateral) to purchase a hot dog cart. Within five years they opened, owned, and operated a restaurant named Carl's Drive-In Barbecue, in Anaheim, California. They later opened a couple of smaller, hence, 'Carl's Junior' restaurants - and the 'race' was on. Today their corporate headquarters is located in Carpentaria, California.

"And then or course, lest we forget, Oklahoma's very own Sonic drive-in was started by a man named Troy Smith from Seminole, Oklahoma, in the mid 1950's. The original Sonic sign can still be seen at their location in Stillwater, and their corporate headquarters is still located in Oklahoma City," Chuck concluded.

Joe was now so totally confused that he couldn't finish eating his breakfast. He was trying to figure out if his friend had completely lost his mind, or if at this point he should even be riding in the same car his friend was driving! "With all due respect Chuck, have you lost your mind?" Joe asked. "Did you really just claim that all of those fast food restaurants, founded by different people, in different places, and at different times, featuring different products and practices and places of headquarters, are all part of the McDonalds Corporation? How could that possibly be?"

"It couldn't possibly be, could it Joe? It is actually pretty absurd, isn't it?" Chuck asked.

"It is absurd!" Joe responded. "It's unbelievable! So why would you say such a thing?"

"Well, to illustrate the answer to the question you asked me just before we picked up breakfast. You remember; you asked me if all the different denominational churches weren't really just all parts of the same one body of Christ we see in Scripture. Well, to begin with, the bible says in Ephesians 1:22-23 that the church is the body. Therefore, the church of Christ - the original church as seen purchased, established, and in existence in Scripture - is the body of Christ according to God."

Chuck giggled in spite of himself as he prepared to continue. "Just ask the Baptists, the Methodists, or anyone else who adamantly claims to be just another part of the body of Christ, if they're really a part of the church of Christ, and watch them fall all over themselves contradicting their own claims, since the 'body of Christ' and the 'church of Christ' biblically refer to exactly the same, one, entire, saved by the blood of Christ, New Testament group of undivided, undenominated, pre-denominational people.

"But more importantly, consider this. You just said that it was completely absurd to consider that different entities, started by different people, in different places, at different times, and with different competing practices and headquarters were all just different parts of the one, same, original entity – and you're absolutely correct! General Motors is not part of the Ford Motor Company, and Kia is not a subsidiary of Toyota, no matter how intensely or stubbornly somebody feels the need, for whatever reason, to believe that they somehow are.

"So; how is it even remotely possible, to even begin to convince yourself that the Protestant denomination Martin Luther started in Germany in the 1520's (which at least still honors and follows a few of his teachings) in an attempt to correct Catholicism; the Protestant denomination which King Henry VIII started in 1534 in England according to his own desire for more license and therefore secession from the Roman Pope's control; the Protestant denomination which Robert Browne began in England in 1550; the Baptist Church which was originally established by John Smyth in Holland in 1607; or any of the other man-made denominations began in the past 500 years in various and sundry parts of the world by different, uninspired human beings and featuring differing man-made practices, doctrines, names and headquarters which don't even vaguely resemble the congregations of the churches of Christ we see in Scripture, are yet somehow all just differing parts of the same, one, original church or body of Christ as established in Acts 2, named in Romans 16:16, and seen in existence throughout the remainder of the New Testament scriptures many centuries before any human being ever brought any different, man-made Protestant denominations into existence? How is that thought even remotely possible, Joe?" Chuck concluded. "What was that word you used, Joe... absurd?"

"Yeah, that was it," was all Joe could contribute at that point. He was stunned into silence once again at the stark simplicity of it all! They rode on in thoughtful reflection until Chuck wheeled the car into their workplace parking lot. Exiting the vehicle, Joe grabbed their breakfast bag with its half-eaten contents, intending to deposit it in the proper container; but reading the bag's logo one last time, he knew he'd never see fast food restaurants, automobile companies, or differing and competing, doctrinally-contradicting and man-made denominations as exactly the same – or even one and the same with the one, original church in the bible - ever again!

Chapter Eight Questions for Classroom Discussion

1) What do you think about Chuck's approach to this biblical question concerning the church?

2) Who is someone you can personally think of or relate to, whom you would like to now use this type of common-sense approach on?

3) What other entities, companies, or organizations besides restaurants and automobile manufacturers can you think of to integrate into your discussions with people, which utilize this universal truth that different organizations, adhering to different and often contradictory practices and operating procedures, and formed in different times and places by different leaders, are definitely NOT therefore, part of the same, original, unified and united entity?

4) Discuss what else today's fast-food restaurants and modern-day denominational churches have in common besides the elements listed in the above article (i.e., ever-changing menus being constantly updated to reflect the consumer's desires; competing organizations found on every street corner; etc.), which might be creatively integrated into a biblical discussion.

NOTES

Chapter Nine:

Truly Loving Homosexuals

The doors of the cafeteria exploded open as the small mob of impatient employees burst through them, happy that the quarterly safety meeting had finally concluded so that they could get on with their own Saturday afternoon family activities. Actually, this morning's meeting had been more of a workplace sensitivity and tolerance forum on homosexuality than a "safety meeting." And as was evidenced by the often whispered and almost always sarcastic exiting comments of some of Joe's co-workers, he wasn't sure just how effective it had actually been. He, on the other hand, had always considered himself to be a somewhat tolerant, "live and let live" sort of fellow who had no problem at all allowing others to live as they saw fit, without judging them. And so, this morning's corporate directives would cause no complications for him. It would be interesting though to see what his church of Christ friend Chuck had to say about it on their way home though.

Where was Chuck anyway, Joe idly thought as he slowly made his way out to the parking lot? He hadn't seen him since the meeting ended. As Chuck's car came into view Joe finally caught sight of his friend, who for once, did not seem to be his jovial self, but was just leaning against his car, soberly but deeply staring off into the distance, his mouth moving slightly as he was apparently saying a prayer. [1]

"Hey, Chuck, you alright?" Joe asked as his friend saw him approaching and concluded his prayer.

"Not really, but I'll be okay. God is good," Chuck responded thoughtfully.

"What's the matter?" Joe asked concernedly as he came around the front of the car towards his friend.

"It's just so hard to understand why companies like ours, and actually our culture in general harbors such repulsive, abhorrent, and out and out hatred for homosexuals! It makes me so sad some days."

"Ummm... excuse me? Say again," Joe stammered, now completely confused and wondering if his friend had literally lost his mind. "Were you just in the same meeting I was, or was that your identical twin or clone or something sitting there in your place? Because the meeting I was just in was all about accepting homosexuals and their sexual preferences and practices as normal, and not criticizing or condemning their choice of lifestyle."

"Exactly what I just said Joe; that's just about the most unloving, uncaring, inhuman, and deviant thing one could possibly do – something done only to those you obviously care absolutely nothing about, or even could be said to hate," Chuck said, as Joe's bewilderment now surpassed all previous proportions.

"Let me explain," Chuck continued. "Let's say that you and Julie want to go out for the evening and you decide to leave the girls with Charlotte and I. During the course of the evening, your little four-year-old – who can't swim a stroke - asks us to unlock the backyard gate so she can go inside the fence where our in-ground pool is. So, we do. No one says no; no one stops her; no one reaches out to save her, and so she falls in, goes face down, and drowns. After all, the water looked so inviting and pleasurable, so cool and blue and pretty... and all the movies she'd ever seen pools in had always portrayed them as safe and harmless and oh so satisfying. What would you think of us for that?"

But before Joe could utter an answer, Chuck continued on. "Or, let's say your little six-year-old had been in the bathroom and had brought out a bottle of deadly poison drain cleaner, having decided she wanted to taste it because of the colorful bottle. And we 'loved' her enough to let her. No one stopped her or even attempted to, even though we all knew it would undoubtedly kill her. What would you think of us then?"

"How can you even contemplate such horrible things?" Joe, who had had all that he could stand, suddenly blurted out. "I thought you were my friend! How could you even consider allowing such terrible things to happen to my kids?"

"Please forgive me; just trying to illustrate a very serious truth my friend, that's all," Chuck calmly continued. "Oh, and I forgot one thing; the reason none of my family said anything to either of your girls to stop them from indulging in behavior that we all knew would ultimately destroy them, is because we were under strict orders from you never to tell them 'no.'"

"But why would I do such an insane thing?" Joe cut in.

"Because you 'loved' them too much to ever correct any desires they might've had or decisions they'd made, no matter how harmful, deadly, or destructive; in fact, even though you knew that those desires and decisions would absolutely, inevitably, and ultimately destroy them," Chuck's voice trailed off…

"Have you gone completely nuts?" Joe exclaimed, having heard enough. "That's not love! That's…"

"Hate?" Chuck softly interjected, raising his eyes to lock and level a sad but knowing stare into Joe's eyes. "You didn't seem to think it was a minute ago, but you're right; it's surely not love – not even by the most insane and cruel standard imaginable. And that's the point, Joe. Whether it's you as a parent; us as friends who truly love you and your kids; or we Christians who are to truly love all souls and seek to follow in the footsteps of Jesus; any even remotely responsible person who sees another engaging in behavior which they know without a doubt - because it's based on God's authority - will ultimately destroy such people, must never stay silent, but must always speak up to try to warn and stop them before they destroy themselves. [2] This would be true whether they see a person about to plunge off a bridge and take their life; a small child chasing a ball into high-speed traffic; a person who can't swim about to fall into water way over their head; an unsuspecting person about to take a drink of deadly poison; or, know of a person either foolishly and fatally engaging in, or, supporting others who would engage in, homosexual behavior.[3]

"You see, God has stated throughout the bible that the sin of homosexuality is absolutely abhorrent to Him;[4] that it is a soul-defiling sin, and that those who choose to practice it without repentance, shall never, ever, ever enter into heaven. [5] That is truth; that is fact. [6] That is in fact, a fact, that is forever firmly etched and settled in heaven; [7] and no one, no one on earth no matter how much power they might think, claim, or profess they possess, can ever change – not ever. No matter what laws they pass, excuses they claim, or movies they make. Not the government, the Hollywood elite, nor the homosexual advocacy groups like we heard from today. God laughs at the sheer lunacy of all such feeble attempts to thwart or over-rule His Son, His Word, and His authority. [8]

"Subsequently, true and godly love has never, can never, and will never stay silent and not sound a warning when they see anyone seeking to do that which will ultimately – and especially, eternally - destroy them. [9] It just can't. Jesus didn't; Jesus couldn't! [10] And neither can we as His people."

"I see what you mean," Joe solemnly said. "So… you're not going to stay silent like the seminar said?"

"No," Chuck said. "I can't… and it doesn't matter if I do lose my job over it. I love God and my fellow-man way too much to worry about something as temporary as that. [11] The whole reason Jesus died on that cross was to give us all a new start and a second chance to get and stay right with God. And my God requires far more from His redeemed people than to just act like all the pagans around us who hate homosexuals so much that they are willing to support and just let them continue on down the wide path to eternal destruction by staying silent and not speaking up and warning them. Those of us who truly love God and His lost creation can do no less than to continually sound the warning – and to sound it loud enough to give them the chance to repent, be forgiven, and get right with God while they still can. Our current culture and government is so busy proudly parading their no longer even thinly disguised hatred of homosexuals and ultimately promoting their eternal destruction, that they are now seeking to prevent those of us who truly love them from… well, from truly loving and therefore warning them. What about you, Joe?"

ENDNOTES:

1. **Matthew 6:5-6:** And when you pray, you shall not be like the hypocrites. For they love to pray standing in the synagogues and on the corners of the streets, that they may be seen by men. Assuredly, I say to you, they have their reward. But you, when you pray, go into your room, and when you have shut your door, pray to your Father who *is* in the secret *place;* and your Father who sees in secret will reward you openly.

2. **Romans 13:10-14:** Love does no harm to a neighbor; therefore love *is* the fulfillment of the law. And *do* this, knowing the time, that now *it is* high time to awake out of sleep; for now our salvation *is* nearer than when we *first* believed. The night is far spent, the day is at hand. Therefore let us cast off the works of darkness, and let us put on the armor of light. Let us walk properly, as in the day, not in revelry and drunkenness, not in lewdness and lust, not in strife and envy. But put on the Lord Jesus Christ, and make no provision for the flesh, to *fulfill its* lusts.

3. **Please see: Romans 1:18-32**.

4. **Please see** the *"Divinely-Defined Sin Of Homosexuality,"* Bible Study at **www.Godswordistruth.org**.

5. **1ˢᵗ Corinthians 6:9-10:** Do you not know that the unrighteous will not inherit the kingdom of God? Do not be deceived. Neither fornicators, nor idolaters, nor adulterers, nor homosexuals, nor sodomites, nor thieves, nor covetous, nor drunkards, nor revilers, nor extortioners will inherit the kingdom of God.

6. **John 17:17:** "Sanctify them by Your truth. Your Word is truth."

7. **Psalm 119:89 (ESV):** "Forever, O LORD, your word is firmly fixed in the heavens."

8. **Please see and study Psalm 2:1-12!!!**

9. **Please see Ezekiel 2:1-3:11, 33:1-10**.

10. **Please read for example, Matthew, chapters 21-25**

11. **Matthew 10:24-28**: A disciple is not above *his* teacher, nor a servant above his master. It is enough for a disciple that he be like his teacher, and a servant like his master. If they have called the master of the house Beelzebub, how much more *will they call* those of his household! Therefore do not fear them. For there is nothing covered that will not be revealed, and hidden that will not be known. "Whatever I tell you in the dark, speak in the light; and what you hear in the ear, preach on the housetops. And do not fear those who kill the body but cannot kill the soul. But rather fear Him who is able to destroy both soul and body in hell.

Chapter Nine Questions for Classroom Discussion

1) How does 1st Corinthians 13:6 define and describe divine love?

2) How is modern man's definition of love different from almighty God's, when it comes to what love is and how to respond to those who want to continue to engage in any sin that will cost them their eternal souls?

3) What would happen today, to a person proven criminally negligent in the death of a child because they willfully and knowingly refused to intervene in the fatal situation when they could have easily spoken up and prevented such a needless and tragic death?

   How much worse punishment, do you suppose, will he be thought worthy of, who has stood idly and silently by, without speaking up and sounding a warning when it comes to those who are engaging in behavior which God said will ultimately and absolutely result in their eternal death if they don't repent?

4) Discuss the elements of Romans 1:18-32, relevant to today's liberal, leftist lobby, media, and mindset.

5) Discuss the implications of the second Psalm's message for today's superpowers and their high government officials...

6) Can we as Christians, really afford to just stand idly by, while countless millions of biblically ignorant beings created in the very image of God, indulge in a behavior that we know full-well - based on His all-authoritative and timeless Word - will ultimately cause their eternal death away from Him and His glorious presence?

   What do you plan to do about it the next time you are put in a position where this topic comes up?

NOTES

Chapter Ten:

Fired by Ownership!

"Hey, Chuck, what you reading?" Joe said as he walked up behind Chuck, who had been carefully comparing the manufacturers' listed components printed on the containers of a couple of new depth finders in the sporting goods department.

"Just checking out some fishing stuff," Chuck said as he replaced them back on their rack and reached out to shake Joe's hand. "It's sort of 'standard operating procedure' this time of year while the girls are over 'back to school' shopping. What are you doing here?"

"Same thing," Joe replied. "Hey, speaking of 'standard operating procedures,' did you hear that the company finally fired Frank late this afternoon? Man, what a relief! I'm telling you, that guy made life miserable for more people! He made more work and caused more confusion for his co-workers than you'd have thought one man could ever possibly cause – especially me!"

"How so?" Chuck asked.

"He just wouldn't follow company policy or procedure when it came to anything," Joe said. "His reports were continually being rejected, having to be re-done, needing data properly re-entered according to company policy, and then re-submitted. He was always making our department look bad because he was continually telling the guys over in the warehouse they didn't have to necessarily do things the way management had laid down. He always thought he had a better idea than they did – and it's their company! And the owners are the ones with all the money invested! They are the ones who know best how to most efficiently run the company I would think. I mean, I don't always agree with every policy they put in place, but they are the ones who have the authority to make the rules, and our job is to follow them… or apparently – and rightfully - get fired like Frank."

"Hmmm… Reminds me of an illustration our preacher used in his sermon on biblical authority this past Sunday," Chuck said. "It went something along the lines of, 'Two teams get ready to play baseball. The first batter steps into the box wearing a tennis outfit instead of a baseball uniform; holding a wide cricket bat instead of a much narrower, standard baseball bat; demanding 6 strikes for himself instead of 3; and that all the fielders must keep their eyes closed while he was at bat. He had decided these changes would give him the most comfortable, successful, and enjoyable experience possible that day. Of course he was shocked and dismayed at everyone's 'intolerance' when he was laughed off the field, told he was a fool, and had no authority to change the rules - even if it was for his own benefit and personal enjoyment.' I mean, can you image your favorite major league baseball player who is handsomely compensated by his team's ownership to perform for them according to league rules, seeking to do something as insane as that?"

"No I can't; that's just ridiculous," Joe said, "absurd even! In fact, that's just out and out crazy! He sure wouldn't be in the league very long would he? And he would lose everything!"

Chuck hesitated thoughtfully for a moment, and then continued… "It's not really that difficult a thing to understand is it, Joe? Or… is it? I mean, the point our preacher went on to make Sunday was, why is it, when it comes to something as simple and frivolous as man-devised games, entertainment, and sporting events, that we all subconsciously and without a second thought accept the fact that they all must be conducted in accordance with the rules and standards laid down by the recognized governing authorities of those events? This is true from tee ball, to soccer, to basketball, and every competition on any level one can conceive of; they all have rules. And no one in their right mind would even consider doing something as absurd and 'ridiculous' as to charge those who insist on instituting and competing according to those all-authoritative rules as 'intolerant,' would they? We also see the same essential need to submit to the standards of authority as laid down by the human owners of our places of employment or else get fired like Frank did today, don't we?

"So why is it then, that when it comes to something as vital, eternal, and life-and-death essential as where our souls will be forever sent, that so many people believe they can simply shirk God's all-authoritative standard, the bible, and deny its divinely-given 'standard operating procedures' when it comes to things like sin and repentance, the plan of salvation, spirit and truth worship, eternal life and life in general, and also teach others to do things differently from exactly what the 'manual from Immanuel' states as well?

"And then, to top it all off, why do those very same people so often seem to want to insanely scream 'intolerance' (just like our completely misguided, tennis-attired, cricket-bat carrying baseball player) every time those of us who insist on following God's all-authoritative standard [1] state that both baptism and repentance are essential both for and before salvation occurs? [2] That the so-called 'sinner's prayer of faith' to save one's soul and welcome Jesus into one's heart is never, ever found anywhere, in any account, of any New Testament conversion to Christ and is therefore a completely man-made, vain and futile practice which does not save? [3] That there is only one church, one faith, and one baptism acceptable to God, according to God? [4] That women are not to be 'pastors,' preachers, or even serve as song or prayer leaders or bible class teachers whenever and wherever Christian men are present; and that this is even clarified - in writing no less - as being an absolute command of almighty God? [5] That the church in the bible is always seen as singing God's praise without instrumental accompaniment of any kind and therefore set the standard for us, or a thousand other 'standard operating procedures' as set forth in writing by the Owner of the church, 'which He purchased with His own blood?' [6]

"To be quite 'frank,' it's quite simple. If people refute, refuse, and rebel against God's all-authoritative standard's procedures and teachings long enough, there will come a time when they, like Frank, will exhaust Ownership's patience, and get 'fired' as well! [7] And to tell people that, is neither unloving, judgmental, nor intolerant. In fact, it's the most loving thing we can possibly do, as it gives them a chance to repent and get right with God while they still can. And if those we love enough to try to save want to label us who comprise the Lord's church as unloving, judgmental, or intolerant for teaching and insisting on these timeless truths from God, then so be it, 'for so they persecuted the prophets who were before us.'[8]"

ENDNOTES:

1. **2nd Timothy 3:14 – 17:** But you must continue in the things which you have learned and been assured of, knowing from whom you have learned *them,* and that from childhood you have known the Holy Scriptures, which are able to make you wise for salvation through faith which is in Christ Jesus. All Scripture *is* given by inspiration of God, and *is* profitable for doctrine, for reproof, for correction, for instruction in righteousness, that the man of God may be complete, thoroughly equipped for every good work.

   John 12:48-50: He who rejects Me, and does not receive My words, has that which judges him--the word that I have spoken will judge him in the last day. For I have not spoken on My own *authority;* but the Father who sent Me gave Me a command, what I should say and what I should speak. And I know that His command is everlasting life. Therefore, whatever I speak, just as the Father has told Me, so I speak."

2. **Matthew 28:18-20**: And Jesus came and spoke to them, saying, "All authority has been given to Me in heaven and on earth. Go therefore and make disciples of all the nations, baptizing them in the name of the Father and of the Son and of the Holy Spirit, teaching them to observe all things that I have commanded you."

   Acts 2:38 - 42: Then Peter said to them, "Repent, and let every one of you be baptized in the name of Jesus Christ for the remission of sins; and you shall receive the gift of the Holy Spirit. For the promise is to you and to your children, and to all who are afar off, as many as the Lord our God will call." And with many other words he testified and exhorted them, saying, "Be saved from this perverse generation." Then those who gladly received his word were baptized; and that day about three thousand souls were added *to them.* And they continued steadfastly in the apostles' doctrine and fellowship, in the breaking of bread, and in prayers.

1ˢᵗ Peter 3:20 - 21 (KJV): …Once the longsuffering of God waited in the days of Noah, while the ark was a preparing, wherein few, that is, eight souls were saved by water. The like figure whereunto *even* baptism doth also now save us …

3. **Please see: Matthew 15:7-9; Mark 7:5-13; Galatians 1:6-10; Colossians 2:1-23; & 2ⁿᵈ Peter 2:1-22.**

4. **Ephesians 1:22-23 along with 4:4-6**: And He put all *things* under His feet, and gave Him *to be* head over all *things* to the church, which is His body, the fullness of Him who fills all in all… *There is* one body and one Spirit, just as you were called in one hope of your calling; one Lord, one faith, one baptism; one God and Father of all, who *is* above all, and through all, and in you all.

5. **1ˢᵗ Timothy 2:8-15**: I desire therefore that the men pray everywhere, lifting up holy hands, without wrath and doubting; in like manner also, that the women adorn themselves in modest apparel, with propriety and moderation, not with braided hair or gold or pearls or costly clothing, but, which is proper for women professing godliness, with good works. Let a woman learn in silence with all submission. And I do not permit a woman to teach or to have authority over a man, but to be in silence. For Adam was formed first, then Eve. And Adam was not deceived, but the woman being deceived, fell into transgression. Nevertheless she will be saved in childbearing if they continue in faith, love, and holiness, with self-control.

1ˢᵗ Corinthians 14:33-37: For God is not *the author* of confusion but of peace, as in all the churches of the saints. Let your women keep silent in the churches, for they are not permitted to speak; but *they are* to be submissive, as the law also says. And if they want to learn something, let them ask their own husbands at home; for it is shameful for women to speak in church. Or did the word of God come *originally* from you? Or *was it* you only that it reached? If anyone thinks himself to be a prophet or spiritual, let him acknowledge that the things which I write to you are the commandments of the Lord.

6.   **Acts 20:28**

7.   **Please see Matthew 21:33 – 22:14**

8.   **Please see Matthew 5:10-12**

Chapter Ten Questions for Classroom Discussion

1) Is it truly 'intolerant' to insist that we must function within the standards and guidelines of any given authority if we wish to remain a member in good standing of that particular entity?

2) What happens when we continually, blatantly, and directly disobey either the 'standard operating procedures' of places of employment, or even the black and white speed limit on the roadside sign, posted by the local authorities?

   Why should we expect any different if we willfully, continually, blatantly, and directly disobey the divinely-inspired instructions and commandments of Scripture?

3) How many non-Christians do you know who are sports fans? What other creative and applicable variations of the baseball player in the previous chapter can you personally come up with, to help explain to them the same spiritual truths that the illustration does?

4) Where is the "book, chapter, and verse" reference in the New Testament where even one lost sinner is recorded as having recited the "sinner's prayer" to receive forgiveness of their sins and to welcome Jesus into their heart and thus get saved?

   Where is the "book, chapter, and verse" reference in the God's New Testament "rule book" where it states that baptism is "an outward sign of an inward grace?"

   Being "nowhere to be found" in God's all-authoritative Word and divine roadmap to heaven, discuss how close to that destination they are liable to actually get a person.

   How can use the above in your own personal evangelistic efforts?

5) What does God's divine and all authoritative guideline state in the following verses regarding baptism?

➢ Matthew 28:18-20: _____

➢ Mark 16:15-16: _____

➢ Acts 2:38: _____

➢ Acts 22:16: _____

➢ Galatians 3:26-27: _____

➢ Ephesians 4:4-6: _____

➢ Colossians 2:12: _____

➢ 1st Peter 3:21: _____

6) Discuss from 1st Timothy 2:8-15 how we know that this is not just a cultural or first-century requirement.

7) Discuss from 1st Corinthians 14:33-37 how we know that this is a commandment of God and therefore not an outcome left up to our discussion, discretion, or personal, congregational, or cultural preferences.

8) Please re-read Matthew 22:1-14; John 14:6; and Galatians 3:26-27; and then discuss how everyone showing up improperly attired or "out of uniform" will be eternally "fired" by the Owner at the end.

NOTES

Chapter Eleven:

Give Him the F.A.C.S.!

"Hello," Chuck said as he answered his cell.

"Chuck?" Joe's whispered voice came softly into the earpiece.

"Yeah, what's up… and why are we whispering, Joe?" Chuck answered softly.

"I need some help," Joe continued. "It's Julie's Baptist brother again. He's over here visiting and we got into a bible discussion in the other room. He is insisting that John 3:16 proves that all anyone has to do to be saved is just believe and that's it – nothing else. I know from our bible discussions that that's not quite right, but I don't know exactly where to take him in the bible to prove it. Can you help me out?"

"Sure," Chuck said. "No problem. But first, let me guess: he's using the New International Version, right?"

"Yeah… Hey; how did you know?" Joe asked in a slightly surprised tone. "You got E.S.P. or something?"

"No." Chuck replied. "The N.I.V. is just a very misleading version because those who translated it got their own false doctrines and conclusions craftily embedded into its text. If you look at its 'Preface' you'll find that it's not a "strictly literal" translation like the King James, New King James, American Standard, or English Standard versions are for example. Therefore, instead of John 3:16 saying that those who believe in Jesus SHOULD not perish the way those other, more literal versions of the original Greek indicate, the N.I.V. says SHALL not perish, leaving the impression that belief alone, or faith only, is all that's necessary for salvation. Therefore, instead of correctly indicating that believers in Jesus SHOULD not perish – but leaving open the very real possibility that they still can – the N.I.V., by saying they SHALL not perish, falsely gives the impression that faith alone is all that is required for salvation, and that once someone believes, it is simply impossible for them to 'fall from grace' or lose their salvation ever – despite Galatians 5:4. But anyway, what you need to do is give him the F.A.C.S."

"The facts?" Joe asked.

"No, the 'F.A.C.S.' – the '*Faith Alone Challenge Survey*' as our preacher puts it… that is, if he's convinced he's up to the bible challenge" Chuck chortled. "It's a quick, six-scripture study session that explores and exposes the 'faith alone is enough to save' position as the undeniably false, unbiblical, and soul-damning man-made false doctrine that it truly is. Got a pen and paper?"

"Yessirree," Joe said gleefully.

"Okay; to begin with, have him read James 2:19," Chuck said. "And then ask him if he believes demons will be in heaven; because after all, if 'faith alone' is all that's required for salvation, then that passage undeniably confirms that they will."

"Hey, we've discussed that before!" Joe exclaimed.

"Yes, that's right," Chuck said. "We've discussed this next text as well; Ask him to read James 2:24 – the only place in the entire bible where the phrase 'faith only' occurs – and have him explain to you exactly what God almighty says about 'faith alone' being enough to save… that's always interesting – especially with those of the Baptist persuasion," Chuck chuckled.

"Thirdly, have him turn and read Matthew 7:21-23, and answer why those people, who were completely convinced, convicted, and believed with all their hearts and souls that they were definitely going to heaven, somehow did not. After all, they both obviously believed and confessed Jesus as Lord – the only two things that most denominationalists of his stripe believe, preach, and practice as being the two elements guaranteeing salvation; and yet, Jesus banished and denied them as His! What happened? Well, what does verse 21 indicate was the other, just as essential element in addition to their belief and confession that they absolutely could not go to heaven without?

"Next, have him turn and read the conclusion and response to the first gospel sermon ever preached, as recorded in Acts, chapter 2, verses 36-47 wherein 3,000 people were saved and added to the Lord's church that day. Ask him how it was, that even though they 'believed' Peter's message so strongly that they were "cut to the heart," by the end of verse 37, they still were not saved by the time we get to verse 40? If 'belief alone' was all that was necessary to save them, then what happened? Why were they not saved by the time we reach the end of verse 37 wherein they were clearly shown to have believed? Verse 40 indisputably shows that they still weren't saved when we get there. What else besides their belief, or 'faith only,' was required before forgiveness and salvation was shown as occurring in verses 38-41?

"Fifthly - and this is a more lengthy reading but that's okay, because by this time, unless he is sincerely seeking the gospel truth, he will have become so frustrated by trying to defend his totally indefensible position that he'll probably have gotten angry and opted out of any semblance of further civil conversation anyway – ask him to explain from the three accounts of Saul of Tarsus' conversion in Acts 9, 22, and 26, just how it was that even after Saul's personal encounter with Jesus; his calling Him 'Lord, Lord;' his subsequent belief and obedience to the point of going into Damascus just as he was told to do by Jesus; plus his three days of intense, personal prayer and fasting, that Saul of Tarsus still had to 'call on the name of the Lord' by being baptized (not by repeating or reciting yet another prayer) in order to have his sins forgiven as it so clearly says in Acts 22:16?

"Sixth; while right there reading the account of the apostle Paul before King Agrippa in Acts 26, ask him if he can please explain how it is that in verses 24-28, that even though Paul knew and confirmed with his own mouth that King Agrippa 'believed,' King Agrippa also knew and confirmed with his own mouth, that he himself was still not yet a Christian! Have your brother-in-law explain how that's even remotely possible if all that's required to be saved and become a Christian is belief alone!

"The bottom line is this Joe. I'm guessing that just like most of the rest of the tragically misled 'faith alone is enough to save' crowd, that he too, continually contradicts his own stated convictions by insisting that one who believes must then, in addition, say a prayer in order to get saved. If he truly believes 'faith alone' is enough to save, then ask him why they then always insist on those who have believed must go through the 'work' of saying a prayer before they are truly saved. John 3:16 doesn't say anything about saying a prayer to be saved either, yet they still insist on it. Let me know how it goes, will you Joe?"

"Thanks man! You're a life-saver!" Joe blurted excitedly.

"No, but God is" Chuck responded. "I'll be praying for you. Call me anytime if there's any other Scriptures you need my friend."

Chapter Eleven Questions for Classroom Discussion

1) Discuss the eternally-affecting difference between "shall not" and "should not" as found in John 3:16, depending on whether one uses the "dynamic equivalence" method of translation New International Version, or one of the more "strictly literal" translations such as the King James, New King James, American Standard, or English Standard versions.

2) Where exactly, in each individual bible can one look to find which translation method – dynamic equivalence, strictly literal, or something less – was used to produce it?

3) Discuss and dissect the F.A.C.S.: What is it? What are its components? Explain how committing them to memory can help you evangelistically, and with whom you plan to share them in return.

4) What is the only verse in the entire bible where the phrase "faith only" or "faith alone" occurs? What does it say?

5) Please turn to and prepare to discuss Matthew 7:21-23… Did the people therein "confess with their mouths" and "believe in their hearts" that they were saved as so many denominationalists today claim are the only two requirements to getting saved? Did it work? Why? What did they leave out? Where did they end up?

6) Please turn to and prepare to discuss Acts 2:37-41… At what point did the people mentioned therein actually believe the message they'd heard about Jesus? And yet, how do we know for certain from that very passage, that they were not yet saved - even at the very point they believed?

7) Discuss from Acts 9:9-11 how we know Saul of Tarsus' three days of intense, involved prayer and fasting still

wasn't enough to get him forgiven, according to Acts 22:12-16.

8) How and when does Acts 22:16 then show, without a doubt, what the act of faith is, by and at which time one 'calls on the Name of the Lord' and is immediately and subsequently saved?'

9) Please turn to and prepare to discuss Acts 26:27-28… Did King Agrippa believe the message Paul and the prophets had preached concerning Jesus? Did that make him a Christian? Will such belief in Jesus alone and without any subsequent, appropriate, or obedient acts of faith (Colossians 2:8-12) get anyone's sins forgiven or make them a Christian according to almighty God?

Who do you know who doesn't yet know that?
What will be their eternal abode if you don't tell them?

Chapter Twelve:

Of Coupons, Car-Pools, & Pre-Destination (Cafeteria Style).

Chuck cheerfully took his lunch tray and turned his attention to finding a place to sit. Across the crowded company cafeteria where they worked, he could see an empty seat at the table near his friend Joe, who was busily engaged in a conversation with a couple of their denominational co-workers. As Chuck approached the table, Larry, the little, lovable, local Lutheran and his best friend, Ben the Baptist, both hurriedly finished their meal and hastily made their departure.

"Hey, Chuck, have a seat," Joe said thoughtfully as Chuck approached the table.

"Thanks, think I will," Chuck replied as he sat down his tray. "Seems to be plenty available. Boy, they sure cleared out in a hurry. Couldn't have been anything I said; I hadn't said anything yet," Chuck said with a slight note of sadness in his voice.

"No, but I think they were afraid you were going to," Joe reflectively but respectfully responded.

"Probably so." Chuck agreed. Both Ben and Larry were nice, polite, pleasant, and dependable co-workers and all. But Chuck had had several conversations with both of them in the past regarding things biblical, and it never ceased to amaze him how anyone could claim to love and trust the Lord and His Word so completely as they both did, but then turn right around and believe and practice so many things that ran completely contrary to everything that Christ had taught and commanded! [1] *I wonder what it was this time?* he thought sadly to himself.

As if reading his friend's mind, Joe continued. "They were talking about something called… 'predestination' I think it was. The idea that before anyone's ever born, God has already decided whether or not they're going to be saved or lost, completely aside from anything they will or won't do or decide for themselves. And that once you're 'predestined' by God one way or the other, you can't thwart or change your fate no matter what."

"Does that make sense to you, Joe?" Chuck asked, after saying a short but silent prayer for his lunch.

"I don't really know," Joe stated hesitantly. "They said it was right there in the bible – Ephesians I think."

"Oh yeah. Although the word 'predestination' itself isn't actually in the bible, the word 'predestined' is in there alright – a total of four times between Romans 8 and Ephesians 1 if I remember correctly," Chuck replied. "But certainly not the way they explain it. Joe, do you know what 2nd Peter 3:9 says?" Joe shook his head. Chuck continued. "It says, 'The Lord is not slack concerning *His* promise, as some count slackness, but is longsuffering toward us, not willing that any should perish but that all should come to repentance.' And so, the question becomes, if 'God our Savior, who desires all men to be saved and to come to the knowledge of the truth,' [2] who so loved the *entire* world "that He gave His only begotten Son," [3] were to actually and irreversibly earmark all men before they were ever born for either eternal heaven, or eternal hellfire, how many do you really think this loving, giving, sacrificial God would actually mark for eternal destruction – if it were fully, totally, only and exclusively up to Him, and Him alone, aside from man, as Lutheranism teaches?"

"Well… none I guess… when you put it that way," Joe said.

"Exactly. If their particular false doctrine of predestination were true – which it obviously isn't - that would also make God a 'respecter of persons,' which would violate yet another biblical text." [4]

"But I thought you said the word was in the bible," Joe puzzled.

"It is. But here's how it works in those four texts… Let's say that our company was giving away free coupons or tickets to seats in their luxury box at the stadium this weekend to see the game. All anyone had to do to acquire a ticket was to stop by the office on Friday, sign the sheet, and then pick them up. Coupon holders were entitled to enjoy everything that came with those luxury box seats and there were seats enough for everybody. In other words, the company had 'predestined' us (all of us that is, who would personally choose to take advantage of their free gift and all the perks that accompanied it), to enjoy an incredible time in their luxury box. But that doesn't mean they were forcing or earmarking certain employees for it while disqualifying others. And at the same time, you also know as well as I do that not every employee would choose to take advantage of such a free gift or offer. Some would think it was too good to be true; some would make or would have already made other plans; and some would simply prefer to spend their time in other pursuits. But either way, all of those folks would summarily miss out on what those of us who would choose to go get the tickets on the company's terms were already pre-destined for by so doing.

"Biblical pre-destination works very much the same way Joe. Both Romans 8:28-30 and Ephesians 1:1-12, explain very clearly that those whom God foreknew - or knew beforehand would love Him and choose to trust Him and want to be with Him – He 'pre-destined,' or made an avenue available to, whereby they could be adopted by Him and experience all the blessings and benefits of being a part of His heavenly family. But the initial and ultimate choice as to whether or not to go obtain that free gift and all that God "pre-destined" for those whom He knew beforehand would willingly thus love and accept Him, would still remain totally and completely under their control – it would remain their choice. Do you see, Joe?"

Joe nodded slowly but still somewhat hesitantly. Chuck searched his mind quickly, looking for a more personal analogy that Joe could perhaps better wrap his mind around. Then he continued. "It's the same idea, as say, car-pooling," Chuck said. "This morning when I drove you and Jack in to work, I had pre-determined, or, 'pre-destined,' as the driver and owner of that vehicle, that my car and all of its occupants – everyone who chose for themselves to get into it of their own free will - was coming here. This is where my car was coming - and you guys knew it. But it was still your choice as to whether or not you got into it and chose to become one of those 'pre-destined' to be here."

"Okay," Joe responded thoughtfully, the light of understanding just beginning to pierce his countenance as he slowly continued. "But what about the automobile in your analogy? Surely, it's not as easy as getting into some vehicle that just happens to be headed for heaven," Joe said, somewhat jokingly.

"Quite to the contrary!" Chuck exclaimed instantly and much to Joe's surprise. "Isaiah the prophet spoke of the 'Highway of Holiness' which the Lord God Himself would provide for all of those to travel who would choose to receive, believe, and trust in His coming Messiah. [5] And Jesus, when He came, spoke of Himself as the very vehicle which one needed to get into, in order to successfully travel that straight and narrow 'highway to heaven,' [6] when He said in John 14:6, 'I am the way, the truth, and the life; no man comes to the Father except through Me.' He is the only way to heaven. And we can't obviously get to heaven 'through' Him, if we are unwilling to first get 'in' Him - just like with my car this morning.

"In fact, it is extremely telling to notice the context of both of those chapters wherein the word 'predestined' occurs. They are inundated with the absolute essentiality of being 'in Christ' in order to become one of those 'predestined' to receive and experience all of those heavenly perks and blessings. Romans 8 begins, ends, and is overflowing with verses explaining some of the incredible benefits which we who have chosen to get into Christ have been predestined by God to enjoy as a result of their choice. That, while the word 'in,' relative to those who have chosen to get into Christ and have therefore been predestined by God to enjoy innumerable and incomparable blessings and benefits both here and hereafter, is found nearly two dozen times in two short chapters in Ephesians 1 and 2."

"That's great and all," Joe suddenly and excitedly said, "but if I understand correctly, then I need to know how a person gets into Christ – according to God of course – because I want to go to heaven too!"

"Okay, tell you what," Chuck said. "There's only two places in the entire New Testament where the phrase "into

Christ" occurs, along with the answer as to exactly how to get "into Christ." They are both very simple. They are Romans 6:3-5, and Galatians 3:26-28. [7] Want to get together tonight and take a look at them, Joe?"

ENDNOTES:

1. **John 14:15, 21, 23-24:** "If you love Me, keep My commandments... He who has My commandments and keeps them, it is he who loves Me. And he who loves Me will be loved by My Father, and I will love him and manifest Myself to him." ...Jesus answered and said to him, "If anyone loves Me, he will keep My word; and My Father will love him, and We will come to him and make Our home with him. He who does not love Me does not keep My words; and the word which you hear is not Mine but the Father's who sent Me."

   Luke 6:46-49: "But why do you call Me 'Lord, Lord,' and do not do the things which I say? Whoever comes to Me, and hears My sayings and does them, I will show you whom he is like: He is like a man building a house, who dug deep and laid the foundation on the rock. And when the flood arose, the stream beat vehemently against that house, and could not shake it, for it was founded on the rock. But he who heard and did nothing is like a man who built a house on the earth without a foundation, against which the stream beat vehemently; and immediately it fell. And the ruin of that house was great."

2. **1st Timothy 2:3-4**

3. **John 3:16**

4. **Acts 10:34-35 (ASV):** And Peter opened his mouth and said, Of a truth I perceive that God is no respecter of persons: but in every nation he that feareth him, and worketh righteousness, is acceptable to him.

5. **Isaiah 35:8-10:** A highway shall be there, and a road, And it shall be called the Highway of Holiness. The unclean shall not pass over it, But it *shall be* for others. Whoever walks the road, although a fool, Shall not go astray. No lion shall be there, Nor shall *any* ravenous beast go up on it; It shall not be found there. But the redeemed shall walk *there,* And the ransomed of the LORD shall return, And come to Zion with singing, With everlasting joy on their

heads. They shall obtain joy and gladness, And sorrow and sighing shall flee away.

6.   **Matthew 7:14**

7.   **Romans 6:3-5:** Or do you not know that as many of us as were baptized into Christ Jesus were baptized into His death? Therefore we were buried with Him through baptism into death, that just as Christ was raised from the dead by the glory of the Father, even so we also should walk in newness of life. For if we have been united together in the likeness of His death, certainly we also shall be *in the likeness* of *His* resurrection,

Galatians 3:26-28: For you are all sons of God through faith in Christ Jesus. For as many of you as were baptized into Christ have put on Christ. There is neither Jew nor Greek, there is neither slave nor free, there is neither male nor female; for you are all one in Christ Jesus.

Chapter Twelve Questions for Classroom Discussion:

1) Turn to and study John 14:15-24. Discuss how these verses would apply to someone who says they love and trust the Lord – the same Lord who said that He had provided us with everything we needed to know to stand complete before Him in His Word (2nd Timothy 3:14-4:4; 2nd Peter 1:2-11) – but then would turn right around and attend a church, practice worship, and teach and defend doctrines that are not only foreign to the all-sufficient and authoritative Word of the One they claim to love and want to follow, but are more often than not, found to be quite contrary to it.

2) Describe the common, man-made, modern-day Lutheran and Protestant denominational doctrine of predestination.

   How do we know that that particular doctrine simply cannot be true, based on such specific biblical texts and truths as we find in John 3:16, Romans 2:4-11, 1st Timothy 2:3-4, and 2nd Peter 3:9?

3) What two chapters of the New Testament do we find the four occurrences of the word 'predestined' in?

   If one is going to get in on and be a part of that one, blood-bought group that is 'predestined' for glory, then they must first choose to get "into Christ." How does one do that, and where are the only two texts in all of Scripture where that phrase appears which prove it?

4) What other examples can you think of, besides the two given in this chapter, which would accurately illustrate for others the true biblical definition of predestination?

Chapter Thirteen:

Issuing the Inevitable, Invincible, Divinely-Inspired, Black & White, Biblical Proof Challenge.

(Please note: The following chapter is actually based on a true-life experience which yielded a similar end result)

"Now you wait just a cotton-picking minute!" Jaws, forks, and heads all seemed to jerk, drop, and rise up all at the same exact instant, as Julie, the typically even-tempered, "live and let live" wife of Joe Clevelander suddenly verbally exploded from her seat at the dinner table. She and her husband might have been the dinner guests of their friends the Churchmans, but she had finally had, and heard, enough! A stunned and stiflingly icy silence suddenly settled over the two families seated there, as she unleashed another, very aggressive, religiously-loaded and emotionally-charged volley at her host. "Are you saying that my family isn't saved just because they've never been baptized for the forgiveness of their sins? I will give you to understand that several members of my family attend church regularly - religiously – just not yours! And," she continued tersely, "my twin sister Jessie is a very devout and faithful minister who probably knows her bible just as well – if not better - than you obviously think you do yours. She actually has her master's degree and a doctorate in ministry! What do you have? You work with Joe." Without waiting for a response, she continued to unload her pent-up frustration. "Jessie preached dad's funeral. He died a charismatic – are you saying my dad wasn't saved? She also preaches for the biggest church in the city every Sunday morning… and there's a lot of good, devout, hard-working people who go there. In fact, they have about three times more people than the church of Christ where you go. Are you saying that they're not going to heaven simply because they got saved by saying a prayer instead of being dunked in a tank of water? Really?"

The air was so still you could have heard an 'ant breathe,' as all eyes automatically locked onto Chuck. Inside, Charlotte said a silent prayer for Julie as well as for her husband Chuck. She knew that this was the moment they had both been hoping, praying, and waiting for. After all, they'd been here before. Many times. It always came down to this same sentiment no matter what type or stripe of denominationalist they sought to study with and speak the truth in love to – if said denominationalists were serious about truly seeking a secure salvation relationship with the Savior that was.

As for Chuck, he had to try very hard to hide his elation at his friend's wife's outburst. It was finally time to fight the battle that he simply could not lose; [1] to issue "the challenge" and "lay it right out there on the table" as it were; and to therefore utilize the "spiritual martial arts," or "kung-fu conversion" principle as he preferred to refer to it. You see, Chuck knew that the big secret to most self-defense techniques was to let the adversary lose control and seek to strike first, and then to subsequently respond in such a manner that the former's own strength and momentum could be used to the other's advantage. He also knew that, like Jesus with the woman at the well in John 4, sometimes you had to suddenly change approaches mid-stream and come at some people from a completely different direction without warning, suddenly throwing them totally off-balance. And so, putting all that together, Chuck slowly and lovingly looked up, locking softened, understanding, eyes full of love and compassion [2] with Julie's much more fiery ones.

"Okay, Julie. Point taken. No problem," he said calmly, patiently waiting for his words to sink in. [3] Both Joe and Julie simultaneously took a slow breath – Joe in embarrassment at his wife's uncommon and uncalled for (at least in his opinion) outburst; and she, in cautious disbelief at her host's seeming acquiescence to her statements.

"So, I'm assuming that you grew up in a church with your mom and dad and the rest of the family, where it was preached and taught on a regular basis that a lost person was saved by saying that prayer to have their sins forgiven, and then was to be baptized later, for some other reason… such as 'an outward sign of an inward grace' or something like that. Is that about right?" Chuck asked. Julie nodded. "And that your pastor sister still preaches and teaches that same thing, correct?" Again, Julie nodded, not knowing exactly where this was going, but glad that her husband's best friend finally seemed to be gaining at least some sort of sensitivity when it came to others' salvation and spirituality.

"Tell you what," Chuck said. "We both know that God is not a God of confusion, but of peace. [4] And, we both believe the bible is the absolute truth of God, and we all just want to go to heaven, right?" [5] Julie nodded slowly once again and Chuck patiently continued. "I'll make a deal with you," he said. "If you can show me just one lost soul in the entire New Testament – just one - who was ever saved, forgiven, and converted to Christ by saying that prayer, I will personally, publicly, repent and apologize for every false teaching and thing I've ever said, taught, or even thought regarding the essentiality of baptism for salvation. Additionally, I'll throw out every study, commentary, sermon, and lesson I've ever taught on it. In fact, I'll burn them – and invite you guys over to light and help feed the fire. What do you say?"

"That's it?" Julie replied incredulously, secretly seeking to hide her suddenly elated and inflated sense of satisfaction but all to no avail. "That's all I've got to do?" Her mind immediately raced as she remembered the countless sermons she'd heard growing up – and even from her own sister as an adult - wherein that "sinner's prayer" had been preached, taught, and repeated as the means by, and point at which, one became forgiven of their sins and welcomed Jesus into their hearts and were saved.

"What's the catch? Can't call my sister or anyone if I can't remember all the verses and references myself?" she asked somewhat suspiciously, while trying to hide the hint of sarcasm that also seeped into her voice.

"You can call anyone you want – your sister; the college professors where she got her degree; any member of your family or their pastors and teachers – doesn't matter. You can even call whoever the current head of the Southern Baptist Convention is if you'd like." Chuck said softly. Julie just couldn't believe her ears! This would be like taking candy from a baby! Finally! So, pre-occupied with putting together a mental list of those she believed would be able to point her in the right direction just in case she couldn't immediately put her finger right on the exact verse, she almost missed Chuck's next statement.

"There is one thing though," he said. "If you can't find, out of the thousands of examples of conversions to Christ we have recorded in the Bible since the New Covenant came into effect and Christ's church came into existence in Acts 2, just one, little, measly example of conversion where a lost soul was saved by saying that prayer, then our two families will set down and have a bible study on baptism and salvation. Fair enough?"

"Sure, no problem," she said excitedly. *After all, how hard could it be?* Julie thought to herself as they cleaned up, picked up, packed up, and departed after dinner. *As many times as I've heard that preached, this is going to be a piece of cake – or better yet, a very large piece of 'humble pie' for Mr. C!* she thought to herself.

~~~~~~~~~

It was nearly a month later when Chuck finally caught up with Joe again at work. It was almost as if Joe had been avoiding him for some reason. "Hey, guy, how's it going? Long time, no see!" Chuck said cheerfully as he saw Joe in the hallway. "Haven't heard from you or Julie for several weeks. Charlotte and I were beginning to worry. Everything okay?"

Joe nodded sheepishly. Chuck continued, "Say, did she ever find out anything from her sister regarding that 'book, chapter, and verse' reference from the bible where a lost sinner was saved by saying a prayer, getting forgiven, and welcoming Jesus into their hearts?"

This time, a sheepish headshake in the negative from Joe. "Her sister said she – and I quote – 'couldn't remember where it was found' – unquote. Julie has called several denominational friends and preachers her family knows of and hunted the internet far and wide on church websites. They never give a biblical reference for an example of the sinner's prayer anywhere. But of course, you already knew that, didn't you Chuck?"

Chuck nodded. "I've got a large collection of those little pamphlets our denominational friends and neighbors distribute with their so-called 'plan of salvation' outline in them. Funny thing; they always put in scriptural footnotes for their proof texts after all their other statements, except when they come to the pinnacle; the prayer that they claim supposedly saves a person. When they get there, there's never a biblical footnote following it which shows some lost sinner being saved that way, and we all now know why, don't we, Joe? So, when do we start our bible study on biblical baptism and the salvation it brings?" Chuck asked.

~~~~~~~~~~

That conversation had taken place a little over two months ago. Since that time, Joe and Julie had set with the Churchmans studying the bible on a weekly – and sometimes daily – basis. They had studied all the examples of conversion at length; [6] had all their questions answered with black and white, "book, chapter, and verse" answers; [7] and even begun attending worship with the only church they could find in the bible [8] – the one body, bride, and church, belonging to, headed by, and carrying the all-important and powerful name of, Christ. [9]

And today, as Julie reached out for her husband's hand, they descended the steps of the baptistery together, to finally have their sins forgiven by God, according to God, and to by faith become obedient, cleansed, and blood-bought children of the living God, [10] being added by Him to His church, the moment they were finally, actually, biblically forgiven and subsequently saved; [11] because He deserved to come first, before their parents, grandparents, siblings, friends, or even each other. [12]

ENDNOTES:

1. **2ⁿᵈ Corinthians 10:3-5:** For though we walk in the flesh, we do not war according to the flesh. For the weapons of our warfare *are* not carnal but mighty in God for pulling down strongholds, casting down arguments and every high thing that exalts itself against the knowledge of God, bringing every thought into captivity to the obedience of Christ…

2. **Mark 10:21:** Then Jesus, looking at him, loved him…

3. **Proverbs 15:1-4:** A soft answer turns away wrath, but a harsh word stirs up anger. The tongue of the wise uses knowledge rightly, but the mouth of fools pours forth foolishness. The eyes of the LORD *are* in every place, keeping watch on the evil and the good. A wholesome tongue *is* a tree of life, but perverseness in it breaks the spirit.

    2ⁿᵈ Timothy 2:23-26: But avoid foolish and ignorant disputes, knowing that they generate strife. And a servant of the Lord must not quarrel but be gentle to all, able to teach, patient, in humility correcting those who are in opposition, if God perhaps will grant them repentance, so that they may know the truth, and *that* they may come to their senses *and escape* the snare of the devil, having been taken captive by him to *do* his will.

4. **1ˢᵗ Corinthians 14:33:** For God is not *the author* of confusion but of peace, as in all the churches of the saints.

5. **Please see John 14.**

6. **Please see & study** the *Examples of Conversion Chart* in the appendix of this book.

7. **2ⁿᵈ Timothy 2:15 (KJV):** Study to shew thyself approved unto God, a workman that needeth not to be ashamed, rightly dividing the word of truth.

    2ⁿᵈ Timothy 3:16-4:4: All Scripture *is* given by inspiration of God, and *is* profitable for doctrine, for reproof, for correction, for instruction in righteousness, that the man of God may be complete, thoroughly equipped for every good work. I charge *you* therefore before God and the Lord Jesus Christ, who will judge the living and the dead at His appearing and His kingdom: Preach the word! Be ready in season *and* out of season. Convince, rebuke, exhort, with all longsuffering and teaching. For the time will come when they will not endure sound doctrine, but according to their own desires, *because* they have itching ears, they will heap up for themselves teachers; and they will turn *their* ears away from the truth, and be turned aside to fables.

8. **Romans 16:16:** Greet one another with a holy kiss. The churches of Christ greet you.

    Please see also: the ***Seven Scriptural Names For God's One New Testament Church*** study in the appendix of this book.

9. **Please see Ephesians 1:22-23, 4:4-6, & 5:25-33.**

    Acts 4:12: Nor is there salvation in any other, for there is no other name under heaven given among men by which we must be saved.

10. **Galatians 3:26-27:** For you are all sons of God through faith in Christ Jesus. For as many of you as were baptized into Christ have put on Christ. There is neither Jew nor Greek, there is neither slave nor free, there is neither male nor female; for you are all one in Christ Jesus. And if you *are* Christ's, then you are Abraham's seed, and heirs according to the promise.

11. <u>**Acts 2:36-47:**</u> Therefore let all the house of Israel know assuredly that God has made this Jesus, whom you crucified, both Lord and Christ." Now when they heard *this,* they were cut to the heart, and said to Peter and the rest of the apostles, "Men *and* brethren, what shall we do?" Then Peter said to them, "Repent, and let every one of you be baptized in the name of Jesus Christ for the remission of sins; and you shall receive the gift of the Holy Spirit. For the promise is to you and to your children, and to all who are afar off, as many as the Lord our God will call." And with many other words he testified and exhorted them, saying, "Be saved from this perverse generation." Then those who gladly received his word were baptized; and that day about three thousand souls were added *to them.* And they continued steadfastly in the apostles' doctrine and fellowship, in the breaking of bread, and in prayers... So continuing daily with one accord in the temple, and breaking bread from house to house, they ate their food with gladness and simplicity of heart, praising God and having favor with all the people. And the Lord added to the church daily those who were being saved.

12. <u>**Please see: Deuteronomy 13:1-11; Matthew 4:18-22, 10:32-38, 12:46-50; and Luke 14:25-35...**</u>

Chapter Thirteen Questions for Classroom Discussion:

1) Have you ever been caught on the same end of an emotional outburst such as Chuck was subject to, sitting at his own dining room table? If so, how did your response differ from his? How could you have done better?

2) His initial, immediate, inner reaction to her outburst was one of pure joy. Why?

3) Please describe, in your own words, the *"kung-fu conversion principle,"* as Chuck preferred to refer to it.

4) Please list several reasons and references, as to why he was so confident with this particular approach.

5) What exactly is, in your own specific words, the *"Invincible, Black and White, Biblical Proof Challenge?"*

6) Why is it "invincible?"

7) What would you think of any church leader/preacher/ pastor, who 'forgot' where the example is in Scripture, of a person being saved the same way he teaches one is saved? (Remember, this really happened!) Would you trust such a person to guide, guard, and direct your immortal soul to heaven?

8) Please list by name, at least three people you intend to issue this same *Biblical Proof Challenge* to:

_____

_____

_____

NOTES

Appendix of Seven, Additional, Scripturally-Sound Evangelistic Bible Study Aids for Your Convenience:

Please note that all of the following bible studies and study aids are provided for your personal convenience, and ongoing, personal and congregational, evangelistic efforts. Most of these studies are also available, completely free of charge, in full-sized, 8½ x 11 inch page versions directly from Doug's website at: **www.Godswordistruth.org**, wherein you will also find many other scripturally-accurate bible studies, links, and resources which can be readily accessed and utilized as well.

1. Before We Begin Our Bible Study

2. The Apostles Doctrine Only

3. Two Part, Fourteen Question Pop Quiz for Religious and/or Non-Religious People Wanting and Hoping to go to Heaven

4. Biblical Examples of Conversion Chart

5. What Are **All** the Components that Are **All Absolutely Essential** in Order for One to be Saved?

6. The Seven Scriptural Names for God's One New Testament Church

7. The Kingdom/Church of Christ; Not a Denomination at All! Never Was, Never Will Be!

Before We Begin Our Bible Study...

Before we begin our Bible Study, we need to make sure that we are all in agreement as to the fact that we accept and agree, that the Bible is the Divinely-Inspired, God-breathed, complete and final, all-authoritative, and inerrant Word and will of Almighty God, and the final authority for all things that we accept, believe, and practice; and that as such, it is not to be edited, added to, or taken from; that it does not have an expiration date; and that it is to be absolutely and ultimately trusted above any men's or women's doctrines, feelings, thoughts, and/or experiences; and that it is indeed, the final authority by which we shall be judged, and therefore must abide, as God's children:

- **Deuteronomy: 4:1-2; 5:32-33; 12:28-32; 28:13-14.**

- **Joshua 1:7-9; Psalm 19:7-11; 119:60, 89; Isaiah 55:8-9.**

- **Matthew 4:4; 15:7-9; 22:29 - 31**.

- **Luke 6:46-49.**

- **John 4:23-24; 8:31-32; 12:48-50; 14:15; 17:17**.

- **Romans 3:3-4; 16:17-18**.

- **1st Corinthians 14:37; 2nd Corinthians 4:2; Colossians 3:16; 1st Thessalonians 2:13**.

- **1st Timothy 3:14-15; 2nd Timothy 3:14-4:4; James 1:18 - 21**.

- **1st Peter 1:22-25; 2nd Peter 1:16-21; 3:1-3; 3:14-18**.

- **2nd John 1:1-10; Jude 1:3; Rev. 22:18-19**.

In conclusion then:

If we are truly willing to acknowledge and accept the Bible as the all-authoritative, inerrant, eternal, and abiding Word and Will of Almighty God, and the <u>final authority</u> in all things:

"…that pertain to life and godliness, through the knowledge of him who called us to his own glory and excellence, by which he has granted to us his precious and very great promises, so that through them you may become partakers of the divine nature, having escaped from the corruption that is in the world because of sinful desire. For this very reason, ***make every effort*** to supplement your faith with virtue, and virtue with ***knowledge***, and knowledge with self-control, and self-control with steadfastness, and steadfastness with godliness, and godliness with brotherly affection, and brotherly affection with love. For **if** these qualities are yours ***and are increasing***, they keep you from being ineffective or unfruitful in the knowledge of our Lord Jesus Christ. For whoever lacks these qualities is so nearsighted that he is blind, having forgotten that he was cleansed from his former sins. Therefore, brothers, ***be all the more diligent*** to make your calling and election sure, for if you practice these qualities you will never fall. For in this way there will be richly provided for you an entrance into the eternal kingdom of our Lord and Savior Jesus Christ. **(2ⁿᵈ Peter 1:3-11)**

…then, let us begin our bible study!!!

THE APOSTLES' DOCTRINE ONLY!!!

Our Lord Jesus Christ spoke of the absolute essentiality of living by the whole council – every word - of almighty God (Matthew 4:4). That encompasses *"All Scripture..."* (2nd Timothy 3:16-17). Jesus taught only what God wanted taught (John 7:16-18), and that was God's *truth* (John 8:31-32). *All Scripture is Truth* (John 17:17). And, according to Jesus' own words, our very love for Him is defined by our willingness to obey *His* teaching (John 14:15-23).

But His teaching did not end with His death on the cross. After His death, He would return to His apostles in the form of the Holy Spirit (John 14:15-23), which He did (Acts 2:1-4; 2nd Corinthians 3:17), and continue to reveal and teach God's truth *through* them (John 16:12-14; 17:6-17). What *they* taught was *His* teaching. Incidentally, this is why Jesus could affirm that whatever Peter bound for terms of entrance or admission into Christ's church/kingdom would be honored by Heaven (Matthew 16:18-19). This, because in reality, it would be Christ Himself, His Spirit in Peter, received earlier that day (in Acts 2) that would actually be doing the binding of baptism and repentance for the forgiveness of one's sins. To deny the essentiality of baptism for the forgiveness of sins therefore, is to deny Jesus' teaching, and indeed, Jesus Himself.

This is why it is so vital for us to learn and obey what the apostles taught; for they did not speak from themselves any more than Jesus did during His physical, human existence. He spoke as God directed, and, like the prophets before them, so also did the apostles (2nd Peter 1:20-21). Jesus continued to teach God's absolute truth long after His own earthly death, through His very own hand-picked apostles! For instance, see the following references:

A. Matthew 28:20

B. Acts 2:42, 13:4-12, 18:9-11

C. Romans 16:17-18

D. 1ˢᵗ Corinthians 11:1-2, 14:33-38

E. 2ⁿᵈ Corinthians 4:1-3

F. Ephesians 4:11-16

G. 1ˢᵗ Thessalonians 4:1-8

H. 2ⁿᵈ Thessalonians 2:9-15, 3:6-15

I. 1ˢᵗ Timothy 1:3-11, 4:1-11, 6:3-5

J. 2ⁿᵈ Timothy 1:13, 2:15-19, 3:1-4:4

K. Titus 1:9-2:15

L. Hebrews 2:1-4

M. 2ⁿᵈ Peter 3:15-18

N. 1ˢᵗ John 2:24-27

O. 2ⁿᵈ John 1:6-11

P. Revelation 22:18-19

In ***all*** of these references, we see the importance of teaching ***only*** what Jesus Himself taught, whether in Person, or, ***in the Spirit through His hand-picked apostles, in all things***; not only because it's all we need (2ⁿᵈ Peter 1:3-12, Jude 3), but also because we do not want to face the consequences of denying what Jesus, in the form of the Holy Spirit, directed in the New Testament age, through His apostles (Matthew 12:31-32); that first century faith, "…once for all delivered to the saints" (Jude 3). And if we are not content to teach only what Jesus taught either in Person, or in His apostles' teachings (Acts 2:42), then Scripture says we do not truly love Him (John 14:15), nor is He truly our Lord according to His very own words (Luke 6:46-49).

Fourteen Question Pop Quiz for Religious and/or Non-Religious People Wanting and Hoping to go to Heaven:

STEP ONE: Take the quiz...

1.   Which of the following does the Bible say baptism is?

A). An outward sign of an inward grace.

B). A great and advisable idea for those who have become Christians recently.

C). The very act of faith which now saves you.

D). A symbol of the new life already begun in Christ when one believed.

2.   Which _two_ of the following does the Bible say baptism does?

A). Indicates that one has previously been saved.

B). Places one in Christ.

C). Washes away one's sins.

D). Helps others understand that one has previously become a Christian.

3.   What does Scripture specifically say happens at the exact point someone repents and is baptized?

A). They receive the forgiveness of their sins.

B). They receive the gift of the Holy Spirit.

C). Both of the above.

D). Neither of the above.

4. Which of the following does the Bible say about "faith only?"

    A). Nothing at all.

    B). That it now saves you.

    C). That it's all that one needs in order to be saved.

    D). That it does not save anyone.

5. Which of the following churches are found in the Bible?

    A). Baptist Churches.

    B). Catholic Churches.

    C). Churches of Christ.

    D). None of the above.

    E). All of the above.

6. Which of the below were/are in Christ's earthly kingdom?

    A). Only those who have passed away.

    B). Paul and the Christians at Colossae.

    C). The apostle John.

    D). None of the above - because the earthly kingdom hasn't come yet.

7. Which two below does the Bible state about denominationalism?

    A). That all denominations are okay with God as long as they believe in Jesus.

    B). That those divided and denominated over doctrine are still all part of the one body of Christ despite the different journeys they are on to heaven.

    C). That denominationalism and division are condemned.

    D). That we are all to be of the same one mind and judgment.

8. As we go into all the world and preach the gospel, which of the below will save sinners according to Jesus?

    A). Belief alone.

    B). Belief and repentance.

    C). Belief and worship.

    D). Belief and baptism.

9. In the so-called 'great commission' of Matthew 28:18-20, what two elements did Jesus emphasize as **essential** to the process of making disciples?

    A). A prayer of faith and a sincere heart.

    B). A penitent heart and a willing mind.

    C). Baptism and the continued teaching of Jesus' instructions.

    D). Belief and joining the church of your choice.

10. The bible says in Ephesians 4:4-6 that there is but one body. What are some other terms that would be synonymous for this one body or group of Christ's people?

    A). The church of Christ.

    B). The kingdom of Christ.

    C). The saved of Christ.

    D). All of the above.

    E). None of the above.

11. According to Galatians 5:4, those Christians in the first century church of Christ in Galatia could:

    A). Fall from grace.

    B). Not fall from grace.

    C). Sin so that grace might abound.

    D). Sing and play instruments in worship.

12. Worship must be _____ and not _____ in order to be acceptable to God.

    A). sincere; insincere.

    B). in spirit and truth; according to the teachings of men.

    C). occasional: necessarily every Lord's Day.

    D). attended; done at home with family.

13. Which of the following elements are **never**, **not once**, **ever** found in **any** example of New Testament conversion to Christ we have, of the thousands we have recorded in Scripture, since His church was established in Acts 2?

    A). A prayer of faith welcoming Jesus into one's heart.

    B). Repentance, or the turning of one's heart towards God.

    C). Baptism specifically for the forgiveness of one's sins.

    D). Confession of one's faith in Christ as the Messiah.

14. Which of the following are NOT safe indicators of what God approves of and wants from us?

A). Scriptural Instruction.

B). Our feelings, thoughts, and emotions.

C). New, Holy Spirit inspired and guided revelation.

D). Our consciences.

STEP TWO: Now that you have answered the **Pop Quiz for Religious and/or Non-Religious People Wanting and Hoping to go to Heaven** according to the best of your own knowledge and understanding, please re-take that exact same quiz and answer the questions by first looking up **God's** answers in the following Scriptures (which contain **His** very specific and all-authoritative answers to those exact questions). After completing this second round of the quiz according to God's "book, chapter, and verse" answers, let's compare it to **your** original answers and see how you did.

1.   Galatians 3:26-27, coupled with Colossians 2:12, and fortified especially by 1ˢᵗ Peter 3:21. **(C)**

2.   Romans 6:3-4, and Acts 22:16. **(B, C)**

3.   Acts 2:38. **(C)**

4.   James 2:19-24. **(D)**

5.   Romans 16:16. **(C)**

6.   Colossians 1:13-14, and Revelation 1:9. **(B, C)**

7.   John 17:11-22; 1ˢᵗ Corinthians 1:10; and Philippians 1:27-2:2. **(C, D)**

8.   Mark 16:15-16. **(D)**

9.   Matthew 28:18-20. **(C)**

10. Romans 16:16; 1ˢᵗ Corinthians 12:26-28; Ephesians 1:22-23; Colossians 1:13-24; and Acts 2:47. **(D)**

11. Galatians 5:1-4. **(A)**

12. John 4:23-24, and Matthew 15:7-9 along with Mark 7:6-13. **(B)**

13. See chart on the next page and turn to its references in your bible…**(A)**

14. Acts 26:9-23; Jude 3; Revelation 22:18-19. **(B, C, D)**

If, after you have located God's answers to these questions and compared them to your original ones, and you find that there are any discrepancies, let's please open up the Lord's Word together and discuss and explore them. You see, when we take God at His word and understand that it will be His very and every word (**Psalm 19:7-11, 119:60, 89; 2ⁿᵈ Timothy 3:16-4:4**) – not our thoughts, feelings, consciences, preconceived or previously held notions or teachings (**Matthew 22:29; Acts 26:9-23**) – which will be the sole and all-authoritative source and standard of our soul's judgment on Judgment Day (**John 12:48**)… well then, we understand how important it is to be in compliance with what He said, don't we?

We love you with the love of the Lord and want so much for your soul to be saved on that day, because the absolute truth (**John 8:31-32**) is that many are living their lives believing they are okay with the Lord, when according to that very same Jesus' very own teaching, "many" who believe they are saved and who even confess Him as "Lord" have only deceived themselves, and simply will not be saved because they did not learn, love, live and do His Father's will (**Matthew 7:21-27**). We do not want you to be one of them. Jesus showed that the dividing line between the saved and lost was whether or not the world of people which He loved enough to die for, would respond to His love by loving Him enough in return to live and obey His Word (**John 14:15**). Please, let's discuss that Word as it relates to your answers and how they compare to His right now, shall we?

EXAMPLES OF CONVERSION CHART: ACTUAL "BOOK, CHAPTER AND VERSE" <u>BIBLICAL EXAMPLES</u> OF THE NEW TESTAMENT PATTERN OF CONVERSION TO CHRIST:

Where, Who, How Many?	Heard Gospel	Belief	Repentance	Confession	Baptism	Sinner's Prayer:	Saved?
3,000 People: Acts 2:14-47	22-36	37	38		38-41	<u>Not Found</u>	47
2,000 People: Acts 3:13-4:4	13-26	4:4	3:19, 26			<u>Not Found</u>	4:4
Samaritans: Acts 8:5-13	4-12	12-13			12-13	<u>Not Found</u>	12-13
Eunuch: Acts 8:25-39	35	37		37	38	<u>Not Found</u>	38-39
Saul of Tarsus: Acts 9:3-19, 22:1-16			9:9, 19 22:6-21	22:6-10	9:18 22:16	<u>Not Found</u>	22:16
Cornelius & Household: Acts 10:34-48	34-43	43			48	<u>Not Found</u>	
People Of Antioch: Acts 13:14-48	16-44	48				<u>Not Found</u>	48
Lydia: Acts 16:14-15	14	14			15	<u>Not Found</u>	15
Jailer & Household: Acts 16:30-34	32	31	Contrast vs. 24 with 27-34		33	<u>Not Found</u>	30-34
Isn't it time for YOU to act on God's Word?						<u>Not Found</u> <u>??????</u>	

What Are *All* the Components that Are *All Absolutely Essential* in Order for One to be Saved?

If one were to bake an apple pie, and leave out just one ingredient - the apples, the desired end result would not be accomplished. If a computer company left out just one component –the hard drive; or an automobile manufacturer left out the engine, the end result would be a useless piece of worthless junk. The end result would not be the intended one. What about the importance of attaining the end result when it comes to your desire to be saved?

According to God's Word, the Bible, sinners are saved:

By Belief/Faith in Christ: Luke 8:12, John 3:16, Acts 16:31, Romans 3:22, 1st Corinthians 1:21, Ephesians 2:8.

Through Jesus: John 3:17, 14:6, Acts 4:12, Romans 5:9-10, Hebrews 7:25.

By Calling on His Name: Matthew 28:19, Acts 2:21, 38, 4:12, Romans 10:12-13.

> **NOTE:** The Bible clearly and unquestionably shows, that this is NOT done by saying some prayer that cannot be found in Scripture, but by being baptized, based on faith, into Christ, for the forgiveness of one's sins (Acts 2:38, and 22:16). Biblical Baptism is often referred to in Scripture as "obeying the gospel," which is what the whole point of Romans 10:12-13 is meant, in its natural flow and context, to lead to; see verses 14-21…

By God's Mercy: Titus 3:5.

By God's Grace: Acts 15:11, Romans 3:23-24, Ephesians 2:4-9.

By Being Baptized: Mark 16:16, Acts 2:40-41, 1st Peter 3:21.

- **For** the Forgiveness of Sins: Acts 2:38.
- **To** Receive the Gift of the Holy Spirit: Acts 19:1-5.
- **To** be Saved: 1st Peter 3:21
- **Into** Christ: Romans 6:3-4, Galatians 3:26-27:
  Where _all_ of God's blessings are: Romans 8, Ephesians 1 & 2.

By confessing Jesus as Lord: Matthew 6:14-15, Romans 10:9.

And by obeying Jesus as Lord: Luke 6:46-49, John 14:15.

Some religious teaching omits one or more of the above essential components of biblical salvation, therein contradicting God, Whom, as stated and referenced, said that each and every one of these elements saves you. To say therefore, that any one item/ingredient is expendable, or unnecessary in order to be saved, is to call God's Holy-Spirit dictated Instruction/Word (2nd Peter 1:20-21), a lie, and hence, to perish (Matthew 12:31-32).

Some religious teaching further states that once one is saved, he/she cannot lose their salvation, another blatant disregard and denial of the Word of God (See Galatians 5:4, Hebrews 6:4-6, 10:26-31, & 2nd Peter 2:20-22). We cannot simply stop, with the incomplete picture from above, as some do, to their own destruction.

Therefore, the question becomes: "Once one has been *initially* saved by all of the above listed, what *further* components are vital to *staying* saved (or maintaining their 'saved' status)? For those components *are every bit as vital to being saved in the end* as the above; because God said so too, as noted below. We are saved:

By *loving* the Truth of God's Word: 1st Corinthians 15:2, 2 Thessalonians 2:10, James 1:21.

By _continuing_ in the teaching: 1st Timothy 4:16, 2nd Peter 1:5-11, and chapter 3.

By _living_ a new life, _begun_ at baptism: (John 3:3-5, Romans 6:1-23, 2nd Corinthians 5:17), _**made complete**_ **by a life now lived in obedience to God's teaching:** Mark 8:34-38, Luke 6:46-49, Romans 6:1-18, Galatians 5:16-25, & 1st John 2:3-6; **including:**

- _Doing_ **God's will:** Matthew 7:21-23, Hebrews 10:32-39.
- _Doing_ **good works, which validate our faith:** James 2:14-26, _**and**_ **which validate God's investment in us:** Ephesians 2:10.
- **Loving one another:** 1st John 3:11-4:21.

By enduring _to the end:_ Matthew 10:22, Mark 13:13, Hebrews 10:26-39, Revelation 2 & 3.

All 11 components are completely essential, completing the process of our salvation (Matthew 4:4);

1, 2, 3, or even 10 out of 11, will not do, according to the will of God.

We are saved by them all, according to the Word of God.

The Seven Scriptural Names for God's One New Testament Church

- Acts 20:28 (ESV): Pay careful attention to yourselves and to all the flock, in which the Holy Spirit has made you overseers, to care for the **church of God**, which he obtained with his own blood.

- 1st Corinthians 1:2 (ESV): To the **church of God** that is in Corinth, to those sanctified in Christ Jesus, called to be saints together with all those who in every place call upon the name of our Lord Jesus Christ, both their Lord and ours:

- 1st Corinthians 10:32 (ESV): Give no offense to Jews or to Greeks or to the **church of God**…

- 1st Corinthians 11:16 (ESV): If anyone is inclined to be contentious, we have no such practice, nor do the **churches of God**.

- 1st Corinthians 11:22 (ESV): What! Do you not have houses to eat and drink in? Or do you despise the **church of God** and humiliate those who have nothing? What shall I say to you? Shall I commend you in this? No, I will not.

- 1st Corinthians 15:9 (ESV): For I am the least of the apostles, unworthy to be called an apostle, because I persecuted the **church of God**.

- 2nd Corinthians 1:1 (ESV): Paul, an apostle of Christ Jesus by the will of God, and Timothy our brother, To **the church of God** that is at Corinth, with all the saints who are in the whole of Achaia:

- Galatians 1:13 (ESV): For you have heard of my former life in Judaism, how I persecuted the **church of God** violently and tried to destroy it.

- 1st Thessalonians 2:14 (ESV): For you, brothers, became imitators of the **churches of God in Christ Jesus** that are in Judea...

- 2nd Thessalonians 1:4 (ESV): Therefore we ourselves boast about you in the **churches of God** for your steadfastness and faith in all your persecutions and in the afflictions that you are enduring.

- Romans 16:16 (ESV): Greet one another with a holy kiss. All the **churches of Christ** greet you.

- Galatians 1:22 (ESV): And I was still unknown in person to the **churches** of Judea **that are in Christ**.

- 1st Timothy 3:5 (ESV): For if someone does not know how to manage his own household, how will he care for **God's church**?

- 1st Timothy 3:15 (ESV): If I delay, you may know how one ought to behave in the household of God, which is the **church of the living God**, a pillar and buttress of truth.

- Hebrews 12:22-24 (ESV): But you have come to Mount Zion and to the city of the living God, the heavenly Jerusalem, and to innumerable angels in festal gathering, and to **the assembly (*church*) of the firstborn** who are enrolled in heaven, and to God, the judge of all, and to the spirits of the righteous made perfect, and to Jesus, the mediator of a new covenant...

These seven different names of God's group of saved people, His church (*ekklesia*; Gk. "the called out"), or kingdom, as prophesied in Daniel 2, promised in Matthew 16:13-19, and started as promised by Jesus when Peter bound belief, repentance, and baptism, as "terms of admittance" into God's church, which is comprised of all those thus saved (Acts 2:22-47), are the **only** seven names, given by God, in Scripture, for that church (or "body" as it is also called by Christ) over which Jesus alone is Head (Ephesians 1:22-23, Colossians 1:18, 24), and of which, there is only **ONE**: See Romans 12:4-5, 1st Corinthians 10:17, 1st Corinthians 12:12-27, Ephesians 2:16, Ephesians 4:4-6, Colossians 3:15. Those thus saved and in Christ (Romans 6:3-4, Galatians 3:25-27) were and are, called simply, Christians (Acts 11:26).

And it is far more than just the proper, God-ordained, and Biblical name, which makes a church, a Scripturally-organized, God-ordained, and Biblical church – that's just the beginning. They must also worship completely in accordance with God's will (John 4:23-24, 8:31-47, 17:6-17), not man's (Matthew 15:7-9, Luke 6:46-49, Galatians 1:6-10, 2nd John 6-11). In the first-century, pre-denominational, New Testament church which we see purchased, established, pardoned, and reigned over by our Lord and Savior Jesus Christ, each and every congregation was commanded **to teach** the same God-given and apostle-delivered and recorded doctrine. This with no additions, subtractions, deletions, or changes (Please see Acts 2:42 and Galatians 1:6-10).

The Kingdom/Church of Christ; Not a Denomination at All! Never Was, Never Will Be!

1.	Scripture Reading: Matthew 16:13-19, Acts 2:14-37.

2.	The "church" and the "kingdom" are somewhat synonymous terms. While the term "kingdom" comes from a Greek word meaning "rule, reign, authority, or power," and includes both the heavenly and earthly aspect thereof, Christ's church that originated (or was established/founded) in Acts 2 and is seen throughout the remainder of the New Testament, is indeed, the earthly Kingdom of Christ which was promised and prophesied by the Old Testament prophets of God. Consider:

	A.	Christ Himself used the terms "church" and "kingdom" interchangeably (Matthew 16:18-19), as did the writer of Hebrews (Hebrews 12:22-29).
	B.	Christ was born, to establish and govern, an unending kingdom (Isaiah 9:6-7).
	C.	This kingdom would be established during the reign of the Roman Empire (Daniel 2:40-44).
	D.	When Christ was about to be born, the angel Gabriel announced that His kingdom He was born to establish, rule and reign over would not end (Luke 1:26-33).
	E.	Christ preached during His earthly ministry (as did John the Baptist during the same time) that the Kingdom was very close to being established, _**then**_! (See Matthew 3:2, 4:17, 10:7, and Mark 1:15.)
	F.	This kingdom would be where God's will would be obeyed on earth just as it is in Heaven (Matthew 6:10).

G. By Jesus' own Words, this kingdom (the place where Christ was to have all rule, reign, authority, and power) would come during some of His then, first-century audiences' lifetime (Mark 9:1; Luke 9:27).

H. This Kingdom would need to be "cleaned out," or purged of the evil it would contain *"at the close of the age," __before__* the righteous within it would come into the eternal, heavenly aspect of it (Matthew 13:40-43).

I. This church that would never end (Matthew 16:18), was indeed the kingdom that came during some of His then-disciples' lifetime during the reign of the Roman Empire, when Peter preached the first gospel sermon on the day of Pentecost in 33 AD, as recorded in Acts 2, and thereby opened up Christ's church/kingdom (Acts 2:37-47), just as Jesus had promised and prophesied (Matthew 16:19).

J. Paul and the Christians at Colossae, were shortly thereafter regarded as residents already in Christ's earthly kingdom in the first century (Colossians 1:13-14), as were John and his fellow Christians as well (Revelation 1:6-9). **NOTE:** The absurd and anti-Biblical idea that Christ has not yet set up His kingdom but will one day return to establish and rule His kingdom from a literal, earthly throne is absolutely and ridiculously anti-Biblical: See Jeremiah 22:18, 24-30 and Matthew 1:11 as well as the aforementioned!

K. Paul, John, and the Colossians were in the kingdom, in the first century, because they had been born again of the water and the Spirit, to enter that kingdom (John 3:3-5), which is *precisely*, *exactly*, what Peter bound as "terms of admittance" by the leading of the Holy Spirit (2nd Peter 1:20-21), when He opened up Christ's **one and only, exclusive** New Testament church ("called out"/kingdom/saved/body) in Acts 2:14-47.

3. Matthew 16:16-19: This "rock" is the recognition/ acceptance of Jesus Christ as the Son of the Living God,

and is absolutely essential to becoming a member of His one, New Testament, earthly church/kingdom.

4. Peter bound repentance and baptism _**FOR**_ _**the forgiveness of sins**_ (to be saved) and that made people who responded in obedience to that instruction, forgiven/saved members of His forgiven/saved church/kingdom (Acts 2:38-47), as we see in every case of conversion in Acts.

5. Because Christ has _**all authority**_, we must submit to, trust, and obey _**Him**_, or be forever lost (Luke 6:46-49; Matthew 7:21-23, 15:7-9; Hebrews 5:7-9).

6. Life service, not lip service (Acts 2:42-47).

7. **Identifying marks of Christ's New Testament kingdom/church as seen established and in existence in the Bible:**

    A. Was composed of repentant, baptized (**FOR** forgiveness-Acts 22:16) individuals known simply as "Christians" (Acts 11:26), but known collectively as the "church of God" (1st Corinthians 1:2, etc.), "church of the Living God" (1st Timothy 3:15), "church of the Firstborn" (Hebrews 12:23), and/or congregationally as, "churches of Christ" (Romans 16:16).

    B. Took communion on the first day of the week (Acts 20:7).

    C. Gave of their income on the first day of the week (1st Corinthians 16:1-2), not tithing, or under compulsion, but cheerfully and with whatever amount they had personally decided, between themselves and God (2nd Corinthians 8-9).

    D. Was loving, caring, and deeply committed to one another (Acts 4:32-35; Galatians 6:1-2; and Philippians 2; etc.).

    E. Was joyful in suffering (Hebrews 10:32-39; James 1:2-3; Philippians 4:4-13).

F.   Had elders (Acts 20:17, Philippians 1:1, 1st Timothy 3, Titus 1:5).

G.   Was evangelistic in nature (Matthew 28:18-20, Acts 8, Colossians 1:23).

H.   **All taught the same doctrine** (1st Corinthians 4:17, 7:17, 11:16, and 16:1-2). **And that was the Spirit-directed doctrine of Christ** (John 16:12-14) **as delivered ONLY through His hand-picked apostles; JUST LOOK UP THIS LIST:** (Acts 1:1-13, 2:1-47, 13:4-12, 18:9-11; Romans 16:17-18; 1st Corinthians 11:1-2; 2nd Corinthians 4:1-3; Galatians 1:6-10; Ephesians 4:11-16; 1st Thessalonians 4:1-8; 2nd Thessalonians 2:9-15, 3:6-15; 1st Timothy 1:3-11, 4:1-11, 6:3-5; 2nd Timothy 1:13, 2:15-19, 3:1-4:4; Titus 1:9-2:15; Hebrews 2:1-4; 2nd Peter 3:15-18; 1st John 2:24-27; 2nd John 1:8-11). In all of these references, we see the importance of teaching only what Jesus Himself taught, whether in Person, or in the Spirit through His apostles, in all things; not only because it's all we need (2nd Peter 1:3-12, Jude 3), but also because we do not want to face the consequences of denying what Jesus, in the form of the Holy Spirit, directed in the New Testament age, through His apostles (Matthew 12:31-32).

8.   The church of Christ is over 1900 years old, its name appearing in "Romans" (16:16), which was written by Paul in approx. 57-60 AD, and its practices originating and appearing in "Acts," which was written by Luke in approx. 62-65 AD, as well as throughout the New Testament.

9.   Barton W. Stone, Alexander Campbell, and the rest of their contemporaries in the 1800s, were to their time, what Josiah was to his (2nd Kings 22:1-2, 11-13, 23:21-25). They no more founded or established the church of Christ, than Josiah founded or established Judaism! They simply went back to the Word, and planted God's pure seed (Luke 8:11), which always yields God's desired results, wherever and whenever it is spread (Isaiah 55:6-11).

Our statement, as born-again (buried with Him in baptism *for* the forgiveness of our sins and having therefore received the gift of the Holy Spirit – Acts 2:38) New Testament Christians, and Christians only (Acts 4:12, 11:26; Romans 8:9-17; 1st John 5:11-13):

My name is not important except for the fact that it is now in the Lamb's book of life. I am a grace-saved and forgiven member of Christ's one New Testament body/bride/church/kingdom, which He established and founded through the apostle Peter on the Day of Pentecost, during the first-century reign of the Roman Empire just as it was prophesied in Daniel 2 and recorded in Acts 2, **hundreds** of years before **any man-made, modern-day** denomination **ever** came into existence. I am not a member of any denomination that was founded upon, established by, or worships according to, the teachings and commandments of anyone other than Christ's own apostles, or that was founded or established after 33 AD by anyone else, because that is not what the One I believe to be the Son of the Living God, Who has **all** authority, commanded or authorized. I became a member of that Christ-saved group known individually only as "Christians," and congregationally as the "churches of Christ" (Romans 16:16), when I recognized Christ to be the Son of the Living God, and submitted to His Lordship alone, by repenting and being baptized in His Name (by His authority), **for** the forgiveness of **all** my sins. Based on His Truth, I **know** I am saved (1st John 5:6-12). In gratitude, I am now **devoted** to the apostles teaching, to fellowship, to the breaking of bread, and to prayer. (Acts 2:42). Now… ***WHAT ABOUT <u>YOU</u>?!***

www.ingramcontent.com/pod-product-compliance
Lightning Source LLC
Chambersburg PA
CBHW071548040426
42452CB00008B/1109